An Earthling's Guide to Deep Space

Explore the Galaxy Through the Eye of the Hubble Space Telescope

Carolyn Sumners, Ed.D.
Kerry Handron

McGraw-Hill

New York San Francisco Washington, D.C. Auckland Bogotá
Caracas Lisbon London Madrid Mexico City Milan
Montreal New Delhi San Juan Singapore
Sydney Tokyo Toronto

McGraw-Hill
A Division of The **McGraw·Hill** Companies

Copyright © 1999
Published by Learning Triangle Press, an imprint of McGraw-Hill.

All rights reserved. Printed in the United States of America. Except as permitted under the United States Copyright Act of 1976, no part of this publication may be reproduced or distributed in any form or by any means, or stored in a data base or retrieval system, without the prior written permission of the publisher.

1 2 3 4 5 6 7 8 9 0   KGP/KGP   9 0 3 2 1 0 9 8

ISBN 0-07-021988-5

McGraw-Hill books are available at special quantity discounts to use as premiums and sales promotions. For more information, please write to the Director of Special Sales, McGraw-Hill, 11 West 19 Street, New York, NY 10011. Or contact your local bookstore.

Product or brand names used in this book may be trade names or trademarks. Where we belive that there may be proprietary claims to such trade names or trademarks, the name has been used with an initial capital or it has been capitalized in the style used by the name claimant. Regardless of the capitalization used, all such names have been used in an editorial manner without any intent to convey endorsement of or other affiliation with the name claimant. Neither the author nor the publisher intends to express any judgement as to the validity or legal status of any such proprietary claims.

Acquisitions Editor: Griffin Hansbury
Production Supervisor: Claire Stanley
Editing Supervisor: Donna Muscatello

Graphic design production by Gary Young, Avela Corporation.

Printed and bound by Quebecor/Kingsport.

Preface

The Earthlings Guide is interactive. You're on a cosmic journey with the whole universe spread before you. To see it all, you must explore each special place. How about a cosmic mystery to start your tour?

Peek into the cosmos. What do you see ...
    a star cluster,
    a playground,
    a ghost cloud, graveyard, or galaxy?

Guess what kind of place this is and then look for it as you tour the cosmos. The authors will tell you when you find it.

Table of Contents

Introduction
Welcome to the Universe	1
The Secrets of Starlight	4
Seeing Above the Clouds	6
Through Time and Space	9
Tour Features	10

Tour 1
Playgrounds Briefing	14
Famous Birth Clouds	16
Orion Region	20
Extragalactic Playgrounds	26
Jets	28

Tour 2
Star Hopping Briefing	32
Small Stars	34
Stars in Dust	38
Super Stars	42

Tour 3
Ghost Clouds Briefing	46
Famous Death Shrouds	48
Dying Pairs	58

Tour 4
Graveyards Briefing	64
Supernova	66
Nova	70
Supernova Remnants	72

Tour 5
Cosmic Villages Briefing	78
Exploring Globular Clusters	80
Clusters in Other Galaxies	88

Tour 6
Island Hopping Briefing	96
Famous Spirals	98
Barred Spirals	106
Galaxies with Clusters	112
Galaxies Together	116

Tour 7
In the Distance Briefing	124
Black Holes	126
Quasars	134
Field of Galaxies	136
Gravity Lenses	138

Back Home
Special Places	144
Special People	146
Star Map	152

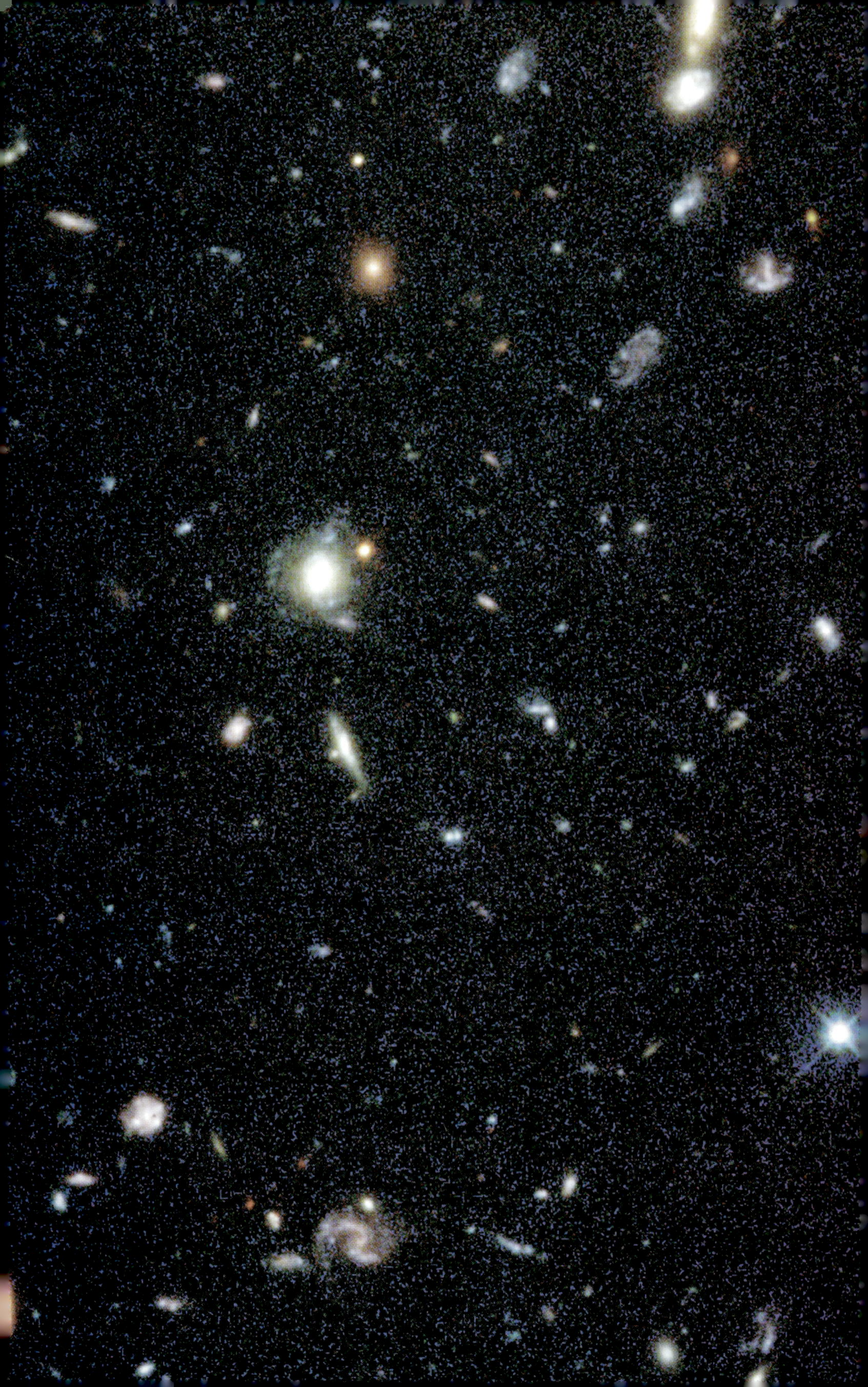

Welcome to the Universe!

You are about to leave Earth on a journey out in space and back in time. Your voyage begins on a small planet, orbiting a middle-aged star, lying in the sleepy suburbs of a large spiral galaxy.

Your destination is deep space among the trillions of stars in the billions of galaxies within view of the orbiting Hubble Space Telescope.

In your journeys, you'll fly past a few objects smaller than Earth – like Earth's moon, the nearby planets, comets, and meteors.

But everything else you see in the night sky is much bigger than your home world.

For instance, the giant planet Jupiter is over 10 times wider than Earth. The Earth could fit inside its Great Red Spot storm.

It would take over a hundred Earths side-by-side to reach across the face of an average star like the sun. The width of a supergiant star, like Betelgeuse, is greater than a thousand Earths. In fact, this star is much wider than the diameter of Earth's orbit around the sun.

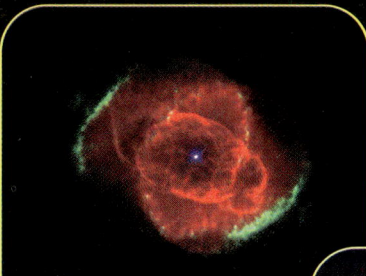

A small cloud of gas and dust surrounding a distant star is much bigger than your whole solar system including the sun and all nine planets.

Large clouds of glowing gas and dark dust are the size of a thousand solar systems and have enough material to make hundreds of stars.

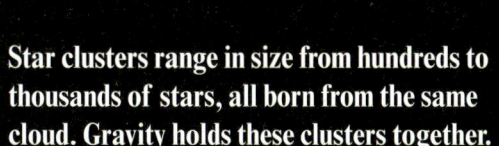

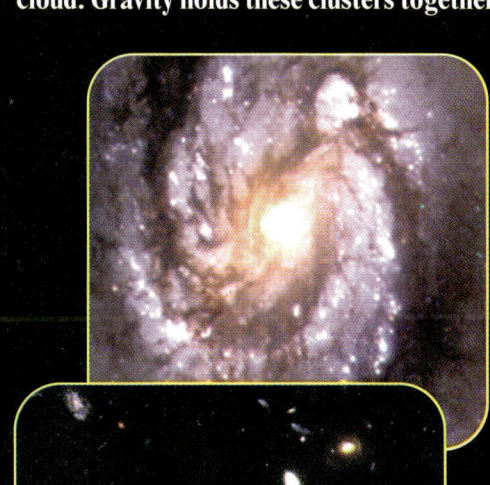

Star clusters range in size from hundreds to thousands of stars, all born from the same cloud. Gravity holds these clusters together.

Galaxies are star systems that range from a million to over a hundred billion stars, plus immense clouds of gas and dust.

Galaxies join in groups which are moving apart as the whole universe expands. This expansion dates back to a cosmic explosion called the Big Bang. Galaxies may continue to drift apart or gravity may someday pull them back together again.

The Secrets of Starlight

Astronomers can't poke a star, crawl around inside it, or take its temperature with a thermometer. The stars are too far away; only their light reaches the Earth. So astronomers put huge telescopes in observatories near the tops of tall mountains – just to capture the most light from distant stars. Then they use cameras attached to computers to collect a star's light. The resulting images turn the computer monitor into a giant window showing the distant universe.

Astronomers can also use a prism or grating to spread starlight into a rainbow spectrum. These colors tell astronomers the star's temperature and identify different gases in the star's atmosphere.

Think about a candle flame. The hottest part near the wick is white while the cooler tips of the flame are orange. A hot blow torch has a blue flame while the embers of a cooling campfire are red. In the same way, a glowing star's color tells you the temperature of its atmosphere. Blue-white stars are the hottest, followed by white, yellow, orange, and red.

You will measure temperatures at different destinations. These temperatures will be in Celsius degrees. The temperatures are so high that you can convert to Fahrenheit degrees by multiplying the Celsius reading by five and then dividing by nine.

Astronomers also identify the gases inside a star by the colors in the star's spectrum. Compare the blue-white light of a bright search light with a yellow street light. The search light contains glowing mercury vapor. Sodium gas produces the yellow in a street light. Red light tubes in outdoor signs contain glowing neon gas. Each element emits its own specific colors.

Notice the colors in the Stingray Nebula. The dying star in the center has produced this cloud of glowing gases. Each color is a different element: nitrogen, red; oxygen, green; and hydrogen, blue.

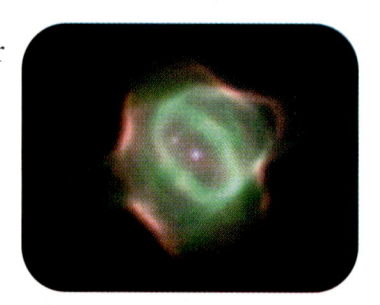

Visible and Invisible Light

Light travels through space in waves, a bit like waves in the ocean. The distance between peaks is the wavelength of the light. Astronomers describe light by its wavelength. You can see only a narrow band of colors ranging from red to violet.

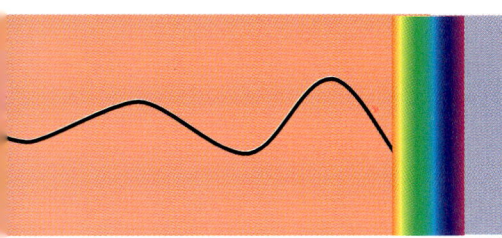

Wavelengths longer than red are called infrared. A remote control sends infrared signals to a television. Warm objects like heaters and humans give off infrared radiation, too. Microwaves have longer wavelengths than infrared. Radio waves, like those your car radio picks up, have the longest wavelengths of all.

Ultraviolet light has a shorter wavelength than violet. It can injure your eyes and give you a sunburn. X-rays have even shorter wavelengths. These waves can penetrate skin and show your bones. They can also destroy cells. Gamma rays have the shortest wavelengths and are the most penetrating of all. These high-energy waves come from very hot objects.

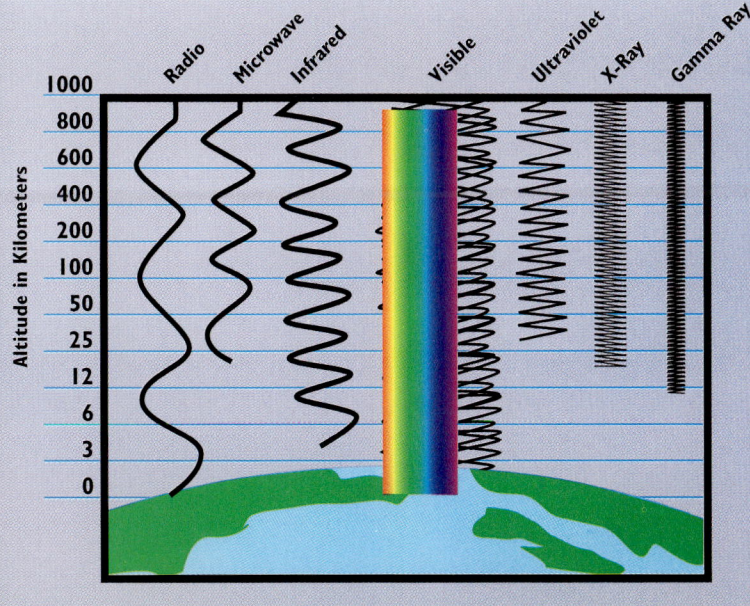

Only visible light and radio waves from space reach Earth's surface. To see the universe in other kinds of light, you must observe above the Earth's atmosphere.

Seeing Above the Clouds

Astronomers have launched satellite observatories to see the universe more clearly and to detect the microwave, infrared, ultraviolet, x-ray, and gamma ray light that is absorbed by Earth's atmosphere. Cool clouds, hot stars, violent explosions, and black holes shine in these invisible "colors."

The largest of the orbiting observatories is a full-sized telescope named the Hubble Space Telescope (HST) to honor Edwin Hubble, the astronomer who first suggested that the universe is expanding. The HST "sees" visible light as well as infrared and ultraviolet radiation. Images from the HST show a universe that is more exciting and beautiful than you can imagine, but far beyond the range of any modern spaceship.

The orbiting Hubble Space Telescope is about the size of a school bus. It's aimed and controlled by astronomers on the Earth's surface. On routine service missions, astronauts from the Space Shuttle repair the HST and install new cameras and other instruments.

Here's how the Hubble Space Telescope works:

Light enters the tube of the HST, strikes the main mirror 2.4 meters wide, bounces from mirror to mirror inside the telescope, and finally reaches the telescope's instruments. The HST can read the lettering on a dime at a distance of over 10 miles and see the light of a firefly about 10,000 miles away. The HST can detect objects that are 50 times fainter and 10 times smaller than any seen from the Earth's surface.

The HST uses solar panels to turn sunlight into electrical power. Images and data from HST instruments are transmitted down to the Earth's surface through the telescope's antenna.

Parts of the HST

A. Main mirror
B. Instruments for collecting data
C. Antenna to relay information to Earth
D. Solar panel for telescope power
E. Screen to protect telescope instruments from sunlight.

Seeing with the Hubble Space Telescope

The Hubble Space Telescope photographs a very small part of the sky. Hold a penny in front of you at arm's length. The HST takes pictures of tiny areas in the sky no larger than the eye of Abraham Lincoln on the penny in your outstretched hand.

The HST has three wide-field cameras and one smaller, more sensitive camera. These four cameras combine to form an image with three large squares and one small square.

Each camera makes an image that is 800 squares (or pixels) wide and 800 squares long.

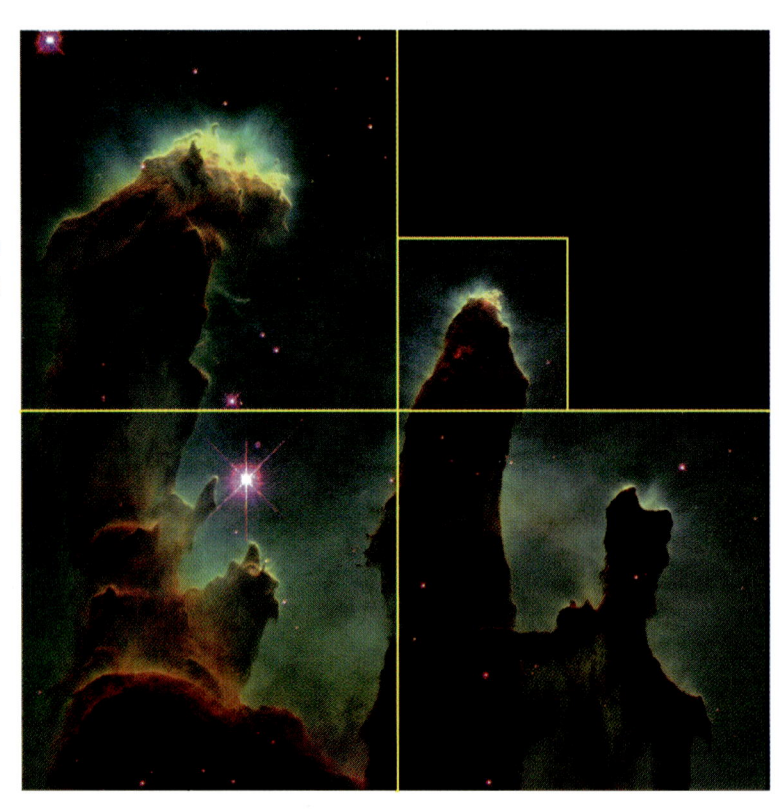

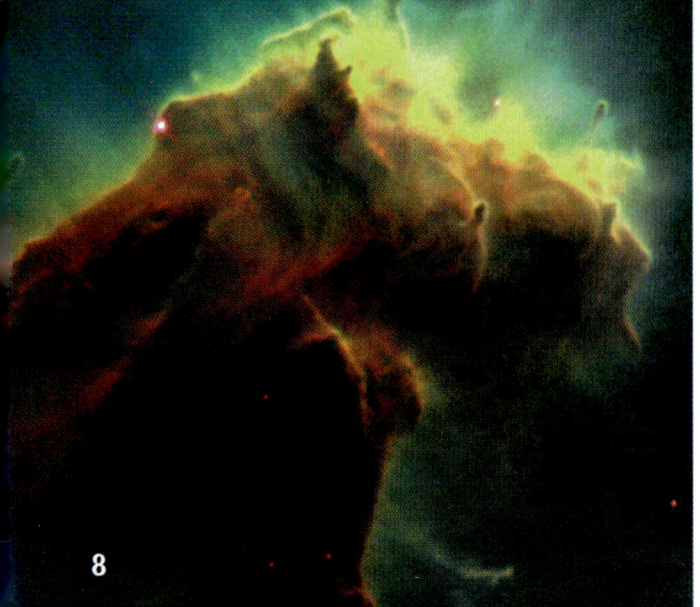

If you enlarge an image enough, you'll see these squares.

These squares represent the actual data that the Hubble Space Telescope collected. You may see these squares or pixels in some of the close-up images on your trip through deep space.

Observing Through Time and Space

Telescopes are really time and space machines. Through them, you see distant objects as they were when their light began its trip toward Earth. Light travels at 186,000 miles (300,000 kilometers) per second. In one year, light covers six trillion miles (9,500 billion kilometers). Light moves so fast that it can circle Earth seven and a half times in a second. But even at this speed, it takes years for light from nearby stars to reach Earth.

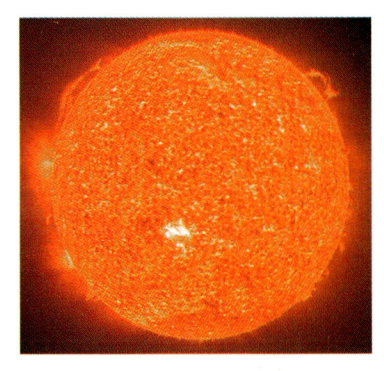

Imagine being outside on a sunny day. It takes sunlight eight minutes to travel from the sun to the Earth. So the sunlight you see is really eight minutes old ... and shows you what the sun was like eight minutes ago. Astronomers say that the sun is eight light-minutes away.

The nearest star to Earth is Proxima Centauri (part of the Alpha Centauri system). Light from this star travels over four years to reach Earth. You see Proxima Centauri as it was over four years ago. Astronomers say this star is 4.3 light-years away. The nearest spiral galaxy to Earth is the Andromeda Galaxy. It is two million light-years away, so you see this galaxy as it was two million years ago.

When the HST takes a photo of a distant object, it captures a moment in the past. This glowing cloud belongs to a galaxy 10 million light years away. Ten million years ago the circled star suddenly became 40 times brighter, making it the brightest star in this galaxy. The HST photographed this ancient event in 1996.

HST images of the most distant objects show events that occurred billions of years ago. There's no way to know how these distant objects look now.

Tour Features: A Star Color Map

In this chart, the brightest objects are on the top and the faintest objects are on the bottom. The hotter blue objects are on the left and the cooler red objects are on the right.

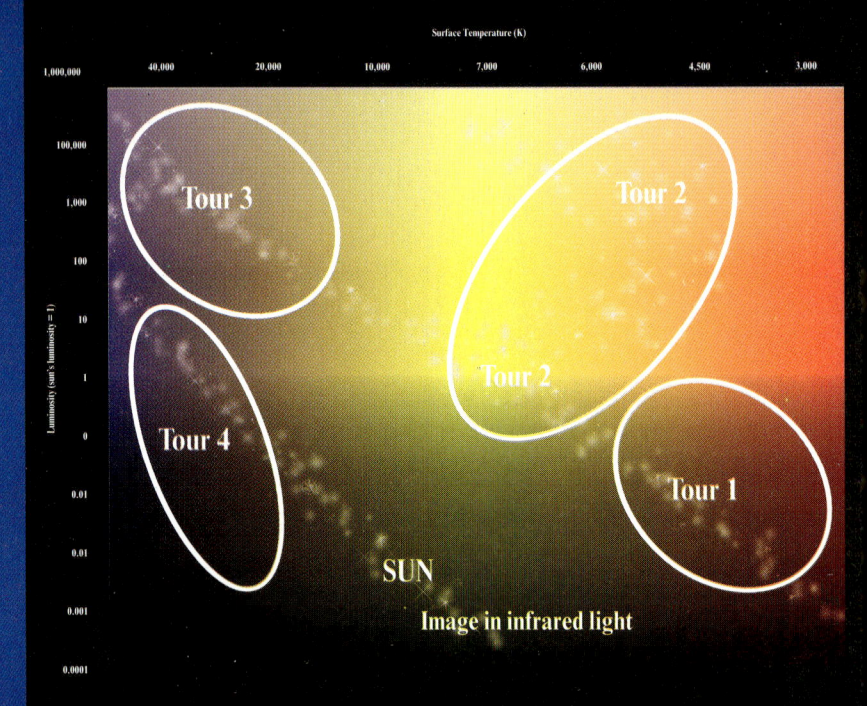

[Star color map diagram showing Surface Temperature (K) on the horizontal axis ranging from 1,000,000 to 3,000, and Luminosity (sun's luminosity = 1) on the vertical axis ranging from 100,000 to 0.0001. Regions labeled Tour 3 (upper left), Tour 2 (upper right and middle), Tour 4 (lower left), Tour 1 (lower right), with SUN labeled. Image in infrared light.]

Your journeys to deep space will carry you all over this star diagram. Each stellar tour begins by locating your destinations on this special map.

In Tour 1, you explore cold, dark clouds in the lower right portion of the diagram. Here bright, hot stars are born.

In Tour 2, you visit middle-aged stars in the middle of the drawing and older stars that have grown into red giants in the upper right.

In Tour 3, you discover that old stars shed their atmospheres in huge shells and reveal their hot, bright inner cores.

In Tour 4, you visit hot, white star cores as well as stars that have shrunk into neutron stars and may explode.

Tours 5-7 feature all these different stars joined together in star clusters, galaxies, clusters of galaxies, and quasars. The entire diagram of stars appear in these tours.

Tour Features: Earth Link

You can plot your course through the star field by using the sky map at the end of this Guide. You will need the LINK TO EARTH data for each destination.

The LINK TO EARTH readouts show how far you are from Earth in time and in distance. Remember, the light-year (ly) measures both. An object that is 10 light-years away in distance is also 10 years backward in time.

LINK TO EARTH
Distance: 1,400 ly
Constellation: Orion
RA: 5.6 hr
DEC: -5.5 deg
Brightness: 4th mag

The LINK TO EARTH displays the constellation and sky map coordinates for each object. Use the constellation name to find the general area, then plot the exact location with the coordinates. Use the RA number (right ascension) to move left or right on the sky map. Use the DEC number (declination) to move up or down from the line in the middle of the map. The LINK TO EARTH above is for the Orion Nebula, a destination in the Playgrounds Tour. The point where the RA and DEC lines intersect is the location of the Orion Nebula in the constellation Orion.

The LINK TO EARTH also describes the brightness of each object in Earth skies. Use these rules, if you want to look for an object outside in the night sky:

Magnitude range	Viewing
between 0 and 3	you can see the object on a clear night, even near city lights.
between 3 and 6	you can see it if the night is clear and moonless and you are far from city lights.
between 6 and 8	you might find it on a clear, dark night by looking through binoculars.
greater than 8	you'll need a good telescope to see an object this faint.

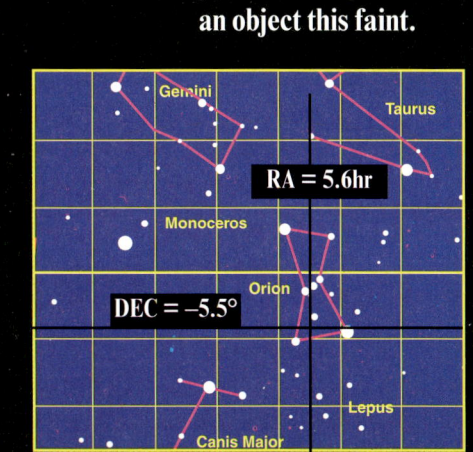

The Orion Nebula has a magnitude of four, so you can see it outside on a clear, dark night when the constellation Orion is visible.

Tour Features: On-Board Movies

Your Earthlings Guide shows flipbook movies along the left blue border of each page. Just flip the Guidebook while watching the left pages to see the action. Some movies carry you around an object. Others show how the object has changed over millions of years.

Feature Flip A   begins on page 14
- Zoom in on the Orion Nebula, the most famous playground of the stars in Tour 1.

Feature Flip B   begins on page 14
- Find the planet circling Beta Pictoris – a highlight of Tour 2, the Star Hopping Cruise.

Feature Flip C   begins on page 14
- Watch as a star ends its life in a supernova explosion – Earth astronomers watched this supernova in 1987.

Feature Flip D   begins on page 66
- Tour the debris from the 1987 star explosion – a favorite Cosmic Graveyard in Tour 4.

Feature Flip E   begins on page 68
- Look for the beeps of the Crab Nebula Pulsar – the most famous cosmic lighthouse on Tour 4.

Feature Flip F   begins on page 126
- Eighteen star clusters come together to form a galaxy in the distant early universe in Tour 6.

Feature Flip G   begins on page 80
- Fly into a galaxy's core to find a monster black hole. Share this adventure in Galaxy Tour 7.

Feature Flip H   begins on page 110
- Travel far away to a quasar in the center of a newborn galaxy. Explore the quasar yourself in Tour 7.

Tours

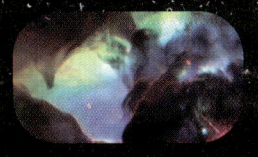

Stellar Tours

Star Tour 1: Playgrounds page 14
Fly through the most famous birth clouds and search for the young stars hiding inside.

Star Tour 2: Star Hopping page 32
Discover the different stars that light the universe – from bright blues to faint reds.

Star Tour 3: Ghost Clouds page 46
Explore the colorful glowing shells thrown off by dying stars.

Star Tour 4: Graveyards page 64
Investigate what happens when a star explodes in a violent supernova.

Galaxy Tours

Galaxy Tour 5: Cosmic Villages page 78
Watch swirling clusters with hundreds or thousands of individual stars.

Galaxy Tour 6: Island Hopping page 96
Visit galaxies of all shapes and sizes as they were millions of years ago.

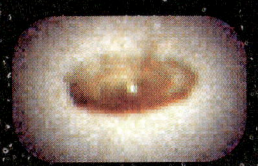

Galaxy Tour 7: In the Distance page 124
Search galaxy cores for black-hole tunnels and for mysterious quasars billions of years old.

Tour 1
Play-grounds

Connection

Stellar playgrounds are enormous clouds of gas and dust lit by energy pouring from newborn stars within. On this tour you'll discover how stars begin their lives.

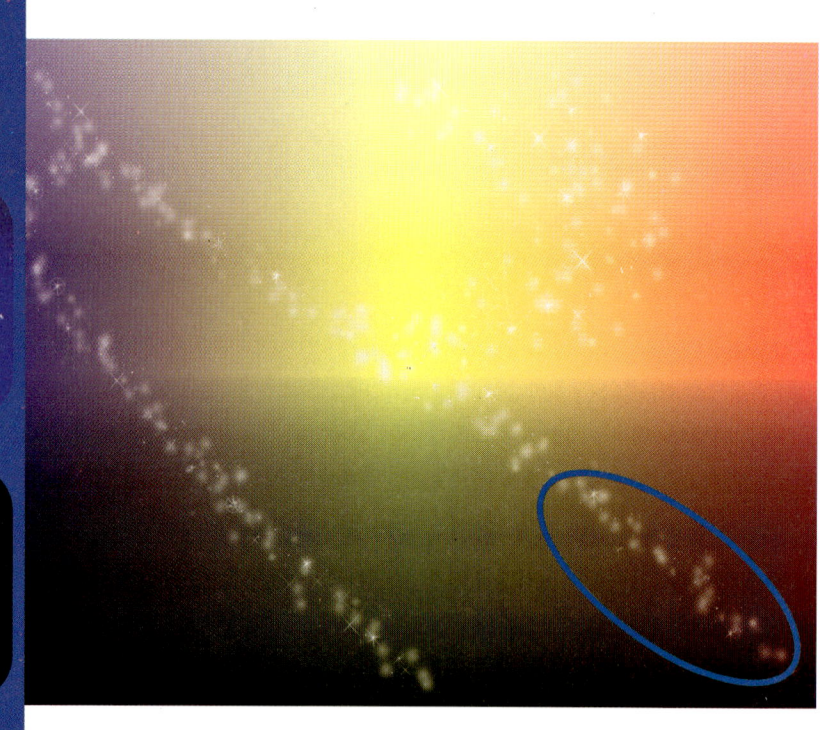

Stellar birth clouds are dark and cold. As newborn stars form, they become very bright and then they settle down to their adult brightness. Most adult stars live in the lower-right part of the star diagram.

Playgrounds

Tour Briefing

On this tour, you'll visit the galaxy's most famous playgrounds like the Eagle Nebula shown above. To find the baby stars here, you must fly around the cloud's dark central pillars.

All suns and solar systems come from gas and dust like this. As dark blobs in the cloud contract, they heat up and begin to glow.

Each year about ten new stars form in dusty regions of the Milky Way Galaxy.

Eagle Nebula
(M16)

LINK TO EARTH
Distance: 7,000 ly
Constellation: Serpens
RA: 18:18 hr
DEC: -13.6 deg
Brightness: 6.5th mag

Did You Know

that these great columns of cold gas and dust are called "elephant trunks"? This is the tallest trunk – about a light-year (or 6 trillion miles) long.

Approaching
New stars form on tentacles extending from the Eagle Nebula's central pillars. These baby stars hide in dark EGGs — or "evaporating gaseous globules." EGGs are really cocoons for newborn stars.

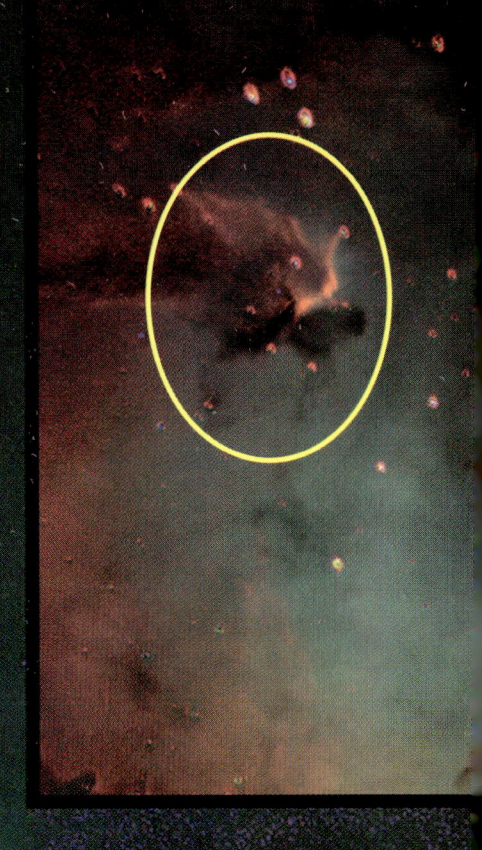

Up Close
Wind blowing from bright stars behind and above you carves these giant columns. As wind erodes these pillars, the round dark EGGs are left behind. Finally the EGGs break off and evaporate and the new stars inside appear.

Look carefully. Some EGGs look like tiny bumps on the surfaces of the gas pillars. Others are joined to columns by a bridge of gas. The bridges survive in the dark shadows of the EGGs.

Lagoon Nebula
(M8)

LINK TO EARTH
Distance: 5,000 ly
Constellation: Sagittarius
RA: 18:03 hr
DEC: -24.4 deg
Brightness: 6th mag

Did You Know

that bright newborn stars cause this strange cloud to glow? The hot center star, called Herschel 36, has blown away the surrounding cool dark clouds to create a bright hourglass shape in the nebula's center.

Approaching

Watch as light from hot stars causes the surfaces of these dark clouds to evaporate in a blue "mist." Violent stellar winds of charged particles also tear into the dark, cool clouds and reshape them.

Up Close

Dark twisters descend into the cavern. These funnels and twisted ropes surround the heart of the Lagoon Nebula. Large temperature changes occur between the hot surfaces and cold interiors of these clouds. These temperature differences and the pressure of starlight cause the strong winds that twist these clouds into tornadoes.

Orion Nebula
(M42)

LINK TO EARTH
- Distance: 1,500 ly
- Constellation: Orion
- RA: 5:35 hr
- DEC: -5.3 deg
- Brightness: 4th mag

Did You Know

that from Earth, you can see the Orion Nebula just by looking up on a clear winter night? It looks like a misty patch in the sword region of the constellation Orion. In the top flip movie, you can zoom in on this beautiful cloud.

Stars formed here less than 500,000 years ago. The gas cloud is lit by four of the largest and hottest newborn stars.

Approaching

It's hard to believe that one fuzzy patch in Earth's winter sky could be so brilliant and violent. The color of the gas shows what kinds of atoms are here: hydrogen glows green; oxygen, blue; and nitrogen, red.

Up Close

Here very large, hot stars give out so much light that they blow away part of the dust cloud. You're looking down a large tunnel into the heart of this giant cavern ... to four stars called the Trapezium. These brilliant newborn stars are only about 100,000 years old.

This bright pocket lies just inside the huge dark cloud which creates the pocket's sharp edge.

Flowing gas creates a shock wave that turns the cloud into new stars. On the following pages, you'll see these newborn stars up close and explore the dark cloud nearby.

Orion Proplyds

LINK TO EARTH
Distance: 1,500 ly
Constellation: Orion
RA: 5:35 hr
DEC: -5.3 deg
Brightness: 4th mag

Did You Know

that new planetary systems are forming here? Flattened clouds buried here gradually become stars with orbiting planets. The stars within these clouds are about the size of the Sun. The dark disks range from two to seven times the size of your solar system. Earth and the other planets formed from a disk of gas and dust that surrounded the Sun just after its birth.

Approaching

It's time to start hunting for proplyds. These are dark proto-planetary disks that will soon become solar systems. Proplyd clouds look like wind vanes with tails pointing away from the hottest and brightest stars.

Up Close

In many proplyds, you can find the cool, red central star. Rocky planets like Earth and gas planets like Jupiter could also be forming out of the dust in these proplyds.

The dark proplyds are blocking out the light from glowing gas behind them. The bright proplyds are lit up from the side by the brightest stars in the cavern.

Orion Molecular Cloud
(OMC-1)

LINK TO EARTH
Distance: 1,500 ly
Constellation: Orion
RA: 5:35 hr
DEC: -5.3 deg
Brightness: 4th mag

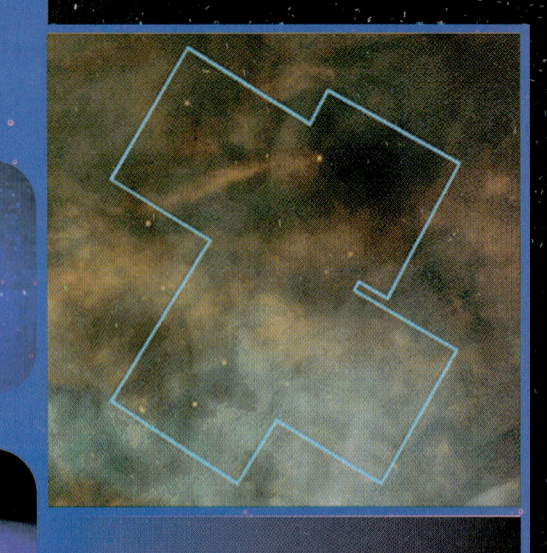

Approaching

The giant dark Orion Molecular Cloud, OMC-1, is featureless in visible light. Light from a few stars in front provides only a hint of the many other stars embedded in this dense cloud. You need infrared filters to see through this cool dust into the active star birth region.

Did You Know

that you are more likely to feel the Orion Molecular Cloud than to see it? The cloud isn't hot enough to glow in visible light. Instead you can see the heat waves from the young stars inside.

Up Close

Through this infrared filter, stars and glowing interstellar dust appear yellow-orange. Excited hydrogen looks blue. Some objects you see here are as small as the Earth's solar system.

The brightest object is a massive young protostar called BN (Becklin-Neugebauer). This star is about to be born.

Blue hydrogen tentacles come from violent outflows of this young star. Outflows may also produce the crescent-shaped "bow shock" on the edge of a dark feature above BN and the two bright arcs below it.

NGC 604
(in M33)

Approaching

The vast nebula called NGC 604 lies in the neighboring spiral galaxy M33. Here new stars are being born in the galaxy's spiral arms. Similar star birth regions lie along the spiral arms of your galaxy.

This cloud is very large — nearly 1,500 light-years across.

LINK TO EARTH
Distance: 2.7 million ly
Constellation: Triangulum
RA: 1:34 hr
DEC: +30.7 deg
Brightness: 10th mag

Did You Know

that this birth cloud lies in another galaxy called M33? This cloud is so huge and brilliant that you can see its light from inside the Milky Way Galaxy.

M33 is very much like your Milky Way Galaxy.

Up Close

You can see over 200 hot stars here. Each is much larger than the sun. These stars are like lanterns in a cavern. They heat the gaseous walls of the cloud and cause the gas to glow.

HH-47

LINK TO EARTH
Distance: 1,500 ly
Constellation: Vela
RA: 8:26 hr
DEC: -51 deg
Brightness: 15th mag

Did You Know

that young stars produce jets streaming out from their poles? These jets remain for only the first hundred-thousand years or so before the hot young stars finally blow away their birth clouds.

Approaching

You can follow the HH-47 gas jet for about half a light-year along the edge of the Gum Nebula. The star making this jet is hidden inside the dust cloud. Look at the twists in the jet. They probably mean that the star inside is wobbling, perhaps moving back and forth as it circles a companion star.

These jets flow into space at a million kilometers per hour. Eventually they hit cooler, denser gas and the collisions cause the gas to glow. At the end of the jets are bow shocks like those produced by a boat speeding through water.

Up Close

Here a jet has burrowed a cavity through the dense gas cloud. Shock waves form when the jet collides with nearby gas. Look at the white filaments. They're reflecting light from a hidden star.

HH-1 and HH-2

Approaching

The HH-1 and HH-2 jets belong to a young star in the constellation Orion. The star is located midway between the jets, but is hidden from view behind a dark cloud of dust.

LINK TO EARTH
Distance: 1,500 ly
Constellation: Orion
RA: 5:35 hr
DEC: -5.3 deg
Brightness: 15th mag

Did You Know

that dark clouds near the Orion Nebula can hide high-speed gas jets? These jets are associated with small, dark blobs called Herbig-Haro or HH objects and they're made by newborn stars.

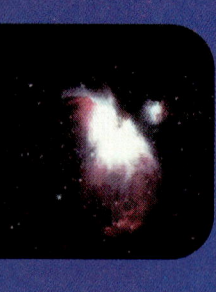

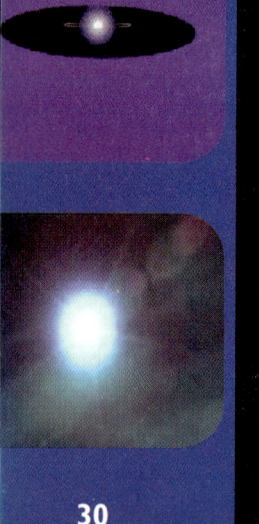

Up Close

These hot jets plow into the cooler gas that surrounds them. Like waves crashing to shore, they form glowing crests in the dark cloud banks.

From end to end, these two jets span more than a light-year. The images in yellow frames are close-ups of parts of these beautiful jets.

31

Tour 2
Star Hopping

Connection

This tour features stars of all sizes and colors – each is special because of its size, age, or surroundings. Soon you'll visit the smallest and largest stars as well as the youngest, oldest, and hottest.

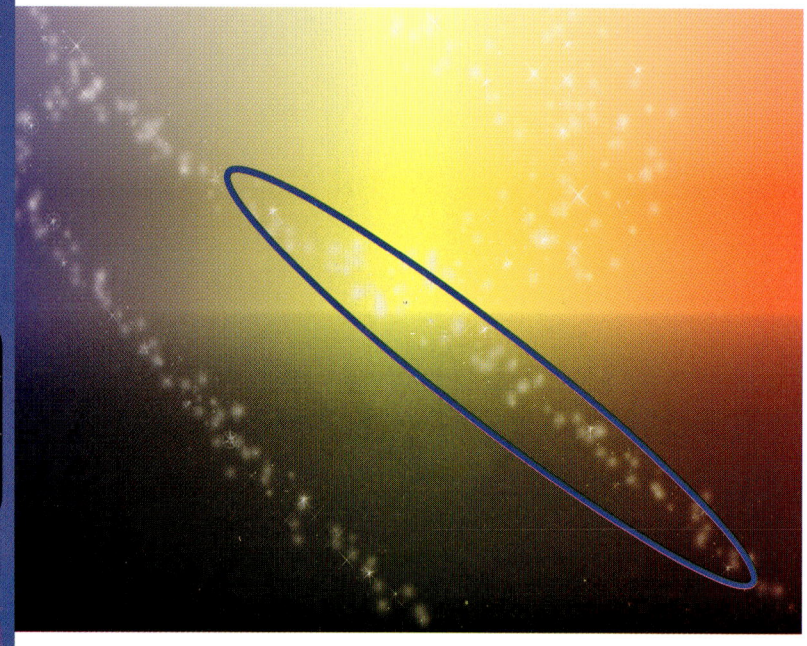

Stars glow in different colors – from blue and white to yellow, orange, and red. Blue stars are the hottest with atmospheres over 10 times hotter than the yellow sun's. Red stars are the coolest. Stars spend 90% of their lives along the stable line in the diagram above. The sun lies in the middle of this line. It's about five billion years old and will live for another five billion years.

In the cores of stars along this line, hydrogen fuses into helium and energy is released in the process. The energy produced in the sun is equivalent to millions of hydrogen bombs going off each second.

Star Hopping

Tour Briefing

Blue stars are the most massive, brightest, and hottest. On average they're 20 times the diameter of the sun, 50 times the sun's mass, and millions of times brighter. They use up their nuclear fuel much faster than the sun and live only a few hundred-million years.

White stars are hundreds of times brighter than the sun, but only about 10 times wider. Their surface temperature reaches 15,000°C. These stars live about a billion years.

A sunlike star is yellow with a surface temperature around 5,000°C. Stars of this size burn steadily for about 10 billion years.

A red dwarf is smaller, cooler, and redder than the sun with a temperature of about 3,500°C. These stars can shine for 100 billion years or more.

In old age, stars grow into red supergiants and spend a few million years in this stage. A red supergiant can be as large as the orbit of Earth or Mars. As stars become supergiants, their expanding atmospheres may swallow inner planets.

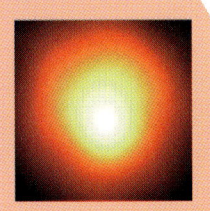

In this tour, you'll travel to nearby red dwarfs with faint companions and to a white star that seems to have planets around it. You'll then visit the hottest blue star known. Your journey ends with the most unstable of all the supergiants visible from Earth.

GL 623B

LINK TO EARTH
Distance: 25 ly
Constellation: Hercules
RA: 16:24 hr
DEC: 48.3 deg
Brightness: 20th mag

Did You Know

that a single star like your sun is unusual? Most nearby stars are pairs of faint red dwarfs.

GL 105C

LINK TO EARTH
Distance: 27 ly
Constellation: Camelopardus
RA: 22.1 hr
DEC: -30.7 deg
Brightness: 19th mag

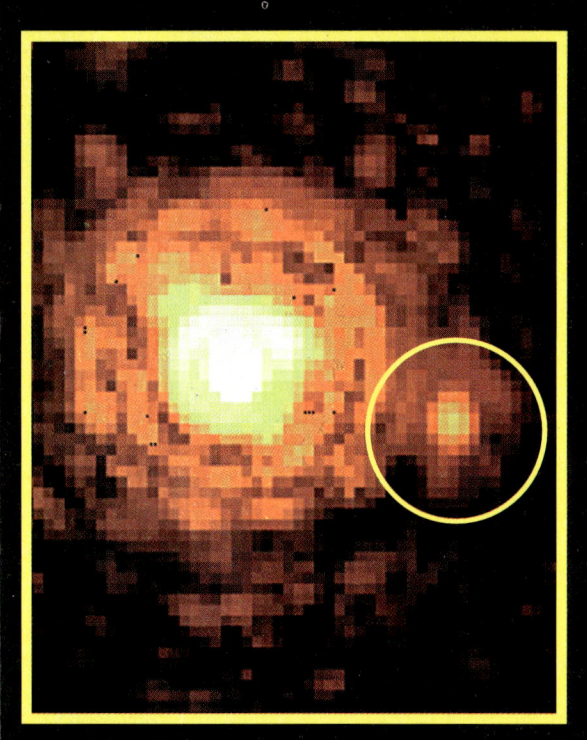

GL623B Up Close

You travel only 25 light-years to reach this tiny rare star. GL623B is one of the smallest stars in the Milky Way Galaxy. It contains about a tenth of the sun's mass and is 60,000 times fainter. GL623B is the smaller component of a double star system where the distance between the two stars is only twice the distance between Earth and sun (about 200 million miles). The smaller star completes one orbit around its larger companion every four Earth years.

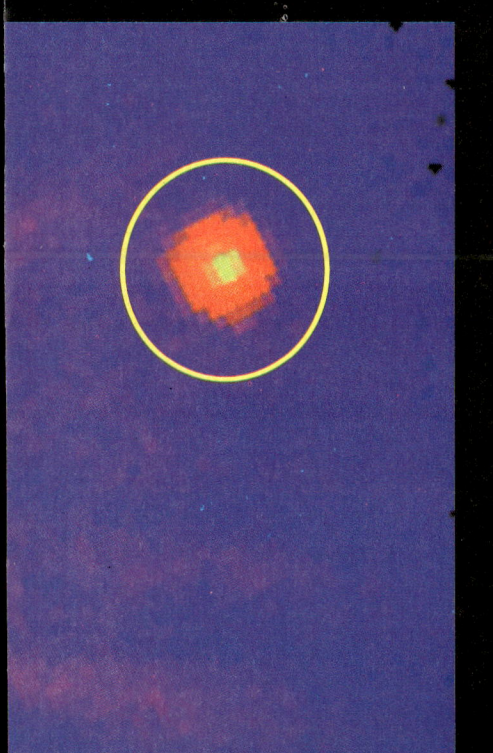

GL105C Up Close

Your second stop is even smaller than GL623B and is also a double star system. GL105C is the tiny companion of a sunlike star called GL105A seen at the lower left. GL105C is 25,000 times fainter than GL105A in visible light. The mass of the small star is less than 9 percent of the sun's mass, placing it near the lower limit for stable hydrogen burning. Objects below this limit are called brown dwarfs. They still "shine"— not by hydrogen fusion, but by shrinking. Diffraction of light inside the Hubble Space Telescope causes the bright spikes on GL105A.

Gliese 229B

LINK TO EARTH
Distance: 18 ly
Constellation: Lepus
RA: 6:11 hr
DEC: -21.8 deg
Brightness: 10th mag

Did You Know

that Gliese229B is one of the faintest objects ever seen around a star beyond the sun? It is definitely not a real star, but a brown dwarf. The brown dwarf orbits the red dwarf star Gliese 229A in a path that is larger than Pluto's orbit around the sun.

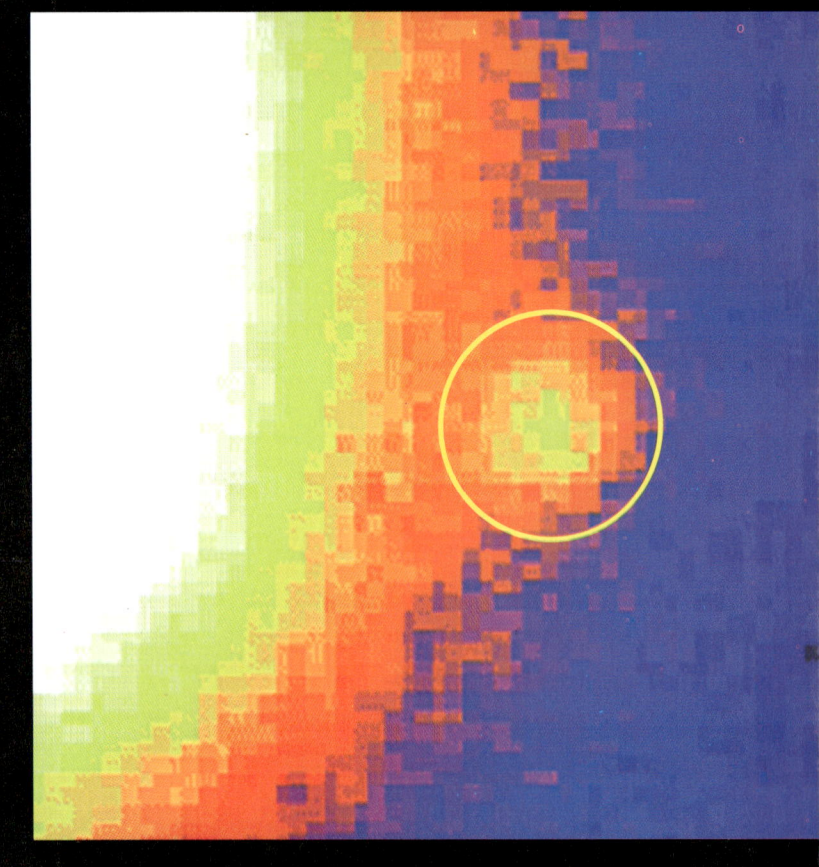

Approaching

Brown dwarfs are mysterious objects that fill the gap between planets and stars. They are far larger than planets, but not large enough to become stars. Gliese 229B is 20 to 50 times the mass of Jupiter, but is about Jupiter's size.

36

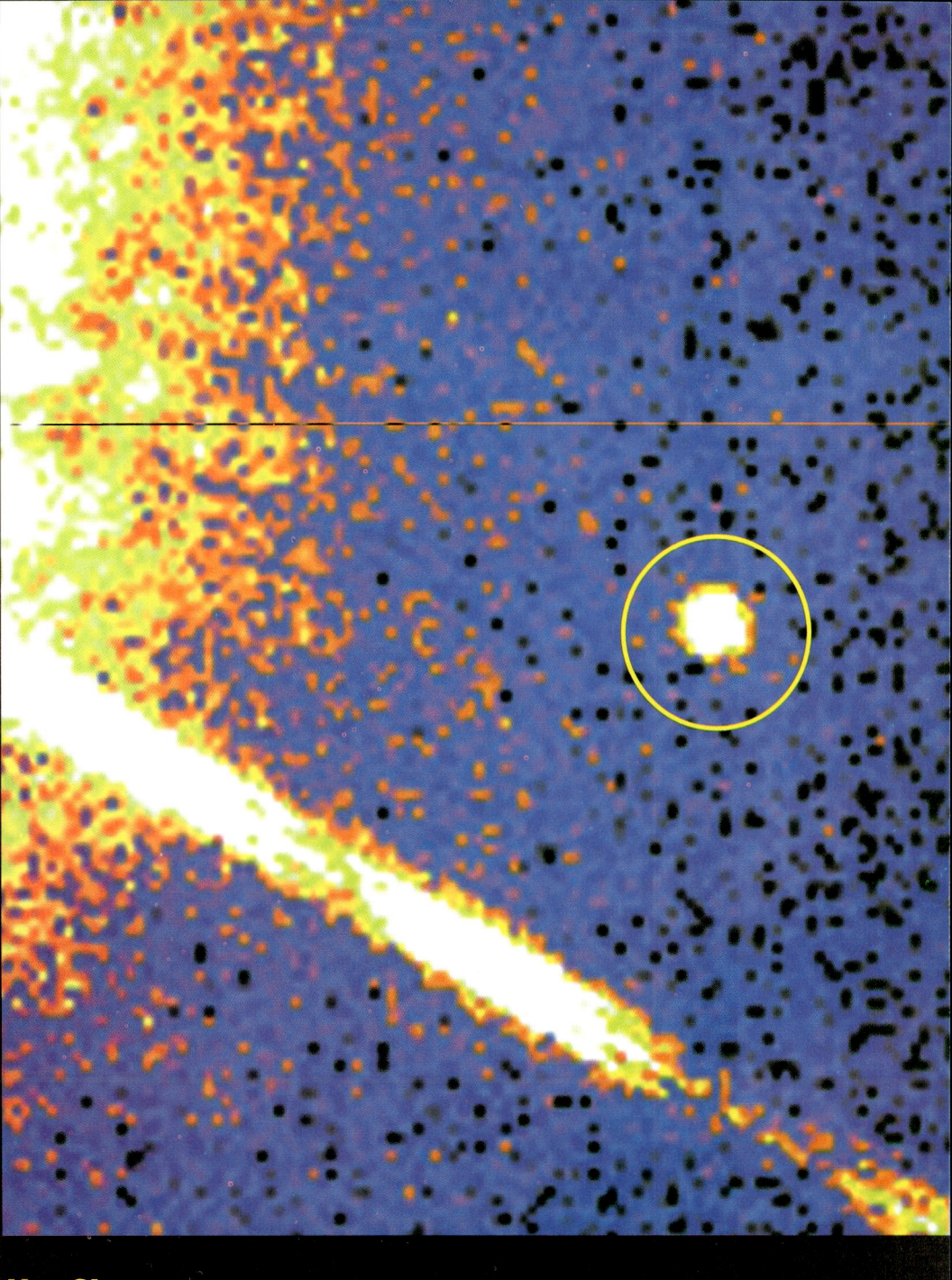

Up Close

This brown dwarf feels warm, but not hot like a regular star. Most of the energy it releases is heat, not light, so you must use infrared filters to "see" it. The red dwarf Gliese 229A is off the edge of the image above, but is so bright that it floods the detector. The diagonal line is a spike from the optical system.

Beta Pictoris

LINK TO EARTH
Distance: 53 ly
Constellation: Pictor
RA: 5:47 hr
DEC: -51.0 deg
Brightness: 4th mag

Did You Know

that astronomers have found a star like the sun surrounded by a solar system in the making? The disk around the star is about 10 times the size of Pluto's orbit around the sun. In the middle flip movie, you can explore this star and the surrounding disk.

Approaching

The disk appears spindle-like because it's tilted nearly edge-on to your view. It's made of ices or sandy particles which reflect light from the star. The central zone around the star is 5 billion miles in diameter and probably contains one or more planets which formed out of the disk.

Up Close

This colorful image brings out details in the disk. The pink-white inner edge tilts slightly to the plane of the outer disk (red-yellow-green) which is marked by a dotted line. There's probably a large planet pulling on the disk. You can't see this planet directly because it's too faint and too close to the star. It is possible that alien life exists in distant solar systems like Beta Pictoris.

NGC 2264 IRS

LINK TO EARTH
Distance: 2,400 ly
Constellation: Monoceros
RA: 6:41 hr
DEC: 10.0 deg
Brightness: 5th mag

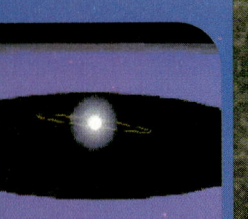

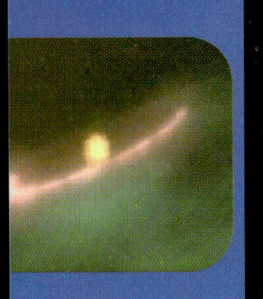

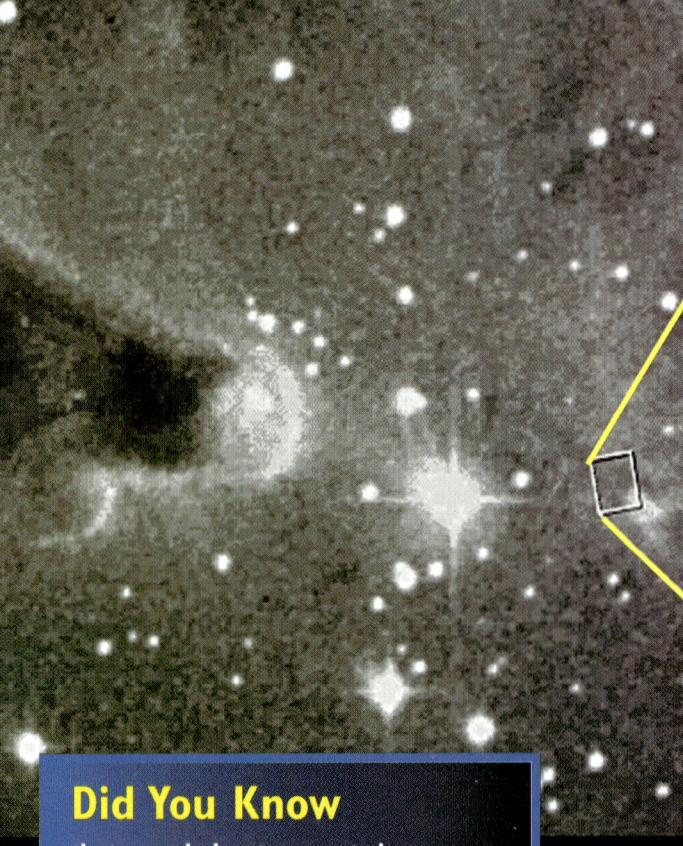

Did You Know

that some baby stars are twins, triplets, or even sextuplets? These six newborn stars are like the sun was five billion years ago. The sun was born alone, but these baby stars were created by the emissions of a very massive star. The large mother star lies in the middle of her six baby suns.

Approaching

A massive star triggered the creation of these baby stars by releasing high-speed particles as it formed. The image to the left shows the Cone Nebula as you approach it from Earth. This stellar birth cloud is like those you visited in the Playgrounds Tour. The white box pinpoints the location of the star nursery where the six newborn suns lie.

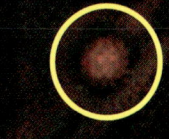

Up Close

Dust and gas obscure the baby stars within. Infrared filters show the heat that these tiny stars produce. Light from the bright mother star inside creates the rings and spikes you see here.

41

Pistol Star

LINK TO EARTH
Distance: 25,000 ly
Constellation: Sagittarius
RA: 17:43 hr
DEC: -28.7 deg
Brightness: 5th mag-dust

Did You Know

that there's a star which is brighter than 10 million suns? It has been nicknamed the Pistol Star. Through an infrared filter, you can see one of the most massive stellar eruptions ever recorded. This brilliant star has enough raw power to blow off two expanding gas shells containing many solar masses of material.

Approaching

One of the brightest stars in the whole Milky Way Galaxy appears as a bright white dot in the center of this image. This star hides at the galactic center behind obscuring dust. You need an infrared camera to penetrate the dust and photograph this star.

Up Close

The largest shell is four light-years wide and would stretch nearly all the way from the sun to the next nearest star. Despite such a tremendous mass loss, this extraordinary star still contains the mass of a hundred suns. In fact it may have started with as much as 200 solar masses of material.

Eta Carinae

LINK TO EARTH
Distance: 8,000 ly
Constellation: Carina
RA: 10:45 hr
DEC: -59.7 deg
Brightness: 6th mag

Did You Know

that the elements in your body were made long ago inside giant stars like Eta Carinae? Over 150 years after the explosion, this expanding cloud is spewing nitrogen, oxygen, carbon, and other elements into space. Long before the solar system existed, giant stars like Eta Carinae lived and died. The elements they formed then became part of the sun and planets.

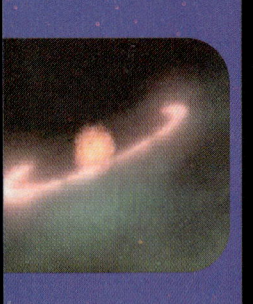

Approaching

You are now approaching one of the largest and most brilliant stars known. Eta Carinae has the mass of 150 suns and is about four million times brighter. This gigantic star can explode violently without warning. The last explosions occurred in 1841, when this star briefly became the second brightest star in Earth's sky (even though it's 8,000 light-years away).

Up Close

Eta Carinae is now growing dimmer, probably because of a bright blue-white dust shell blocking some of its light. Notice the two lobes of material — one moving toward Earth and the other moving away.

Eta Carinae's surface temperature is over 29,000°C. Although the star is hiding now, an explosion is inevitable because of the star's huge size and hot surface. Here eruptions are sudden, violent, and unpredictable.

Astronomers think Eta Carinae could be the next great supernova seen from Earth. And the distant Earth is probably the best place to be when the great explosion occurs.

Tour 3
Ghost Clouds

Connection

In earlier tours you visited huge stellar birth clouds and stars of all sizes and colors. This tour searches for the mysterious ghost clouds that stars create as they die. All of the material in these clouds was once ejected by the star buried within.

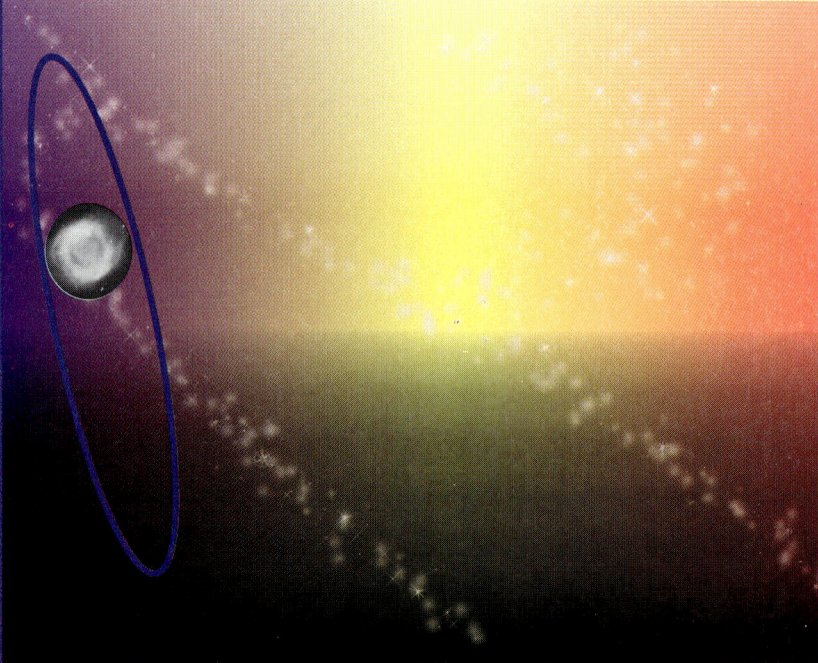

These are the exposed hot cores of dying stars. They lie in the hottest region of the star diagram and mark your destinations in this tour of the galaxy's most famous ghost clouds.

In about 5 billion years the Earth's sun will eject a ghost cloud as it reaches the end of it's stable life.

Ghost Clouds

Tour Briefing

We have known about ghost clouds since the 1800s. Through small telescopes they look like distant planets, so astronomers first named them "planetary nebulas." But these clouds are really much bigger than whole solar systems.

In fact, these ghost clouds lie where solar systems once were. As an old sun dies, it throws off gas shells that were once its outer atmosphere. These shells swallow any orbiting planets. In five billion years, this will be the fate of the sun, Earth, and the solar system.

Your tour path circles each hazy gas shell. Here you will look for new cloud formations and then try to find the hot, dying star which created each cloud.

The two ghost clouds above have bright central stars surrounded by clouds that were once the star's outer layers. NGC 7009 is the larger image and NGC 6826 is the smaller. Energy from the central star causes the outer shells to glow.

Helix Nebula

LINK TO EARTH
Distance: 450 ly
Constellation:: Aquarius
RA: 22:30 hr
DEC: -20.8 deg
Brightness: 6th mag

Did You Know

that you can see the Helix Nebula from Earth? You'll need a small telescope or very large binoculars and a clear, dark moonless night.

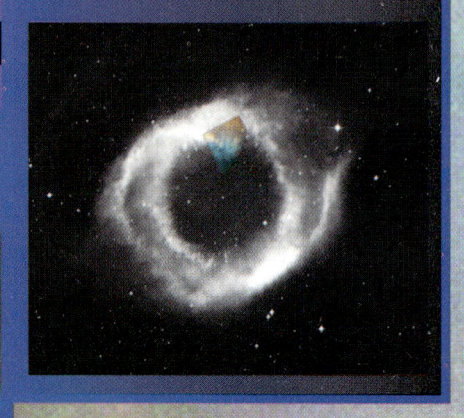

Approaching

At this distance, you can see that the Helix Nebula is really many different gas shells blasted outward by the dying star at the center of the cloud. The central star is above and to your right. Below are strange cloud formations that look like tadpoles swimming in a pond on Earth.

Up Close

You're now on the inside edge of the innermost shell — only a trillion miles from the dying star in the cloud's center.

And you have a great view of the famous gas "tadpoles." Astronomers call them cometary knots because they look like comets with glowing heads and flowing tails. Notice how their tails stream away from the central star like spokes on a wagon wheel.

Here hot gases spewing from the central star crash into cooler gas ejected thousands of years ago. These collisions break up the smooth cloud into small, finger-like droplets, like dripping paint. Each droplet or knot is several billion miles across and very fragile. Wind and light from the central star continuously erode these dusty regions.

NGC 7027

LINK TO EARTH
Distance: 3,000 ly
Constellation: Cygnus
RA: 21:07 hr
DEC: 42.2 deg
Brightness: 10th mag

Did You Know

that this cloud is much younger than the Helix ghost cloud? This star has just begun to throw off its atmosphere. The explosions here are going to be much hotter and more violent as this star faces death.

Approaching

You must move slowly through these wispy, blue cloud streamers. These outer shells were ejected long ago when the central star was still a red giant.

The last violent explosion created the yellow, orange, and red fireball ahead. No one has ever seen the hot core star inside.

Up Close

From this distance, it feels like we're standing on a beach watching huge waves crash to shore. Explosions of the star inside send fast-moving waves of gas outward ... to crash into the older shells above.

Egg Nebula
(CRL 2688)

Approaching

You can see dark, cold dust bands crossing this cloud and strange blue beams piercing the black mist. You'll need an infrared filter to find the warm red gases hiding within the blue-tinged dust.

LINK TO EARTH
Distance: 3,000 ly
Constellation: Cygnus
RA: 21:02 hr
DEC: 36.6 deg
Brightness: 15.5th mag

Did You Know

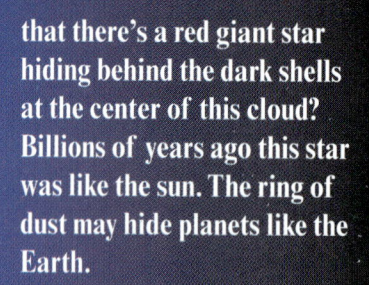

that there's a red giant star hiding behind the dark shells at the center of this cloud? Billions of years ago this star was like the sun. The ring of dust may hide planets like the Earth.

In a distant view, you can tell that these clouds are really shells crossed by dark dust and bright rays.

Up Close

You can count bright bands crossing each glowing egg-shaped cloud. From the spacing of these bands, you can tell that this star throws off gas every 100 to 200 years. These small ejections are part of a larger explosion which has continued for over a thousand years. Dense blobs inside this cloud cast shadows and give the shells a crescent appearance. These dark clouds around the star's equator create the famous egg shapes.

Cat's Eye Nebula
(NGC 6543)

LINK TO EARTH
Distance: 3,600 ly
Constellation: Draco
RA: 17:58 hr
DEC: 66.6 deg
Brightness: 9th mag

Did You Know

that this cloud was named the Cat's Eye because it looks like a cat's eye marble? The Cat's Eye has strange jets, knots, and shells. The jets and knots may be very old. The bright shells are places where gases collide.

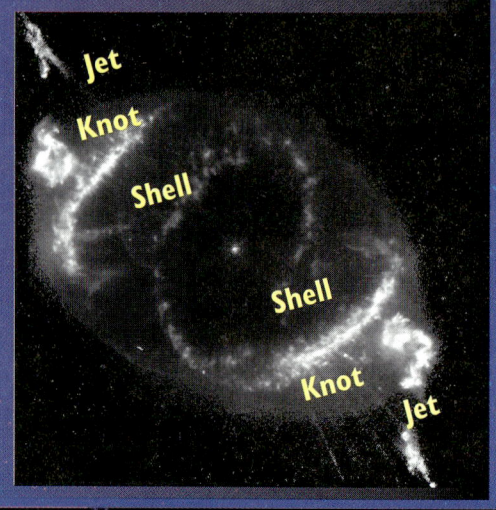

Jet
Knot
Shell
Shell
Knot
Jet

Approaching

You can tell that this violent nebula is very young — only about 1,000 years old. Inside are two central stars. The brighter red giant has shed rings of material in the orbit of its smaller companion sun. The second star inside this cloud may be responsible for the high-speed jets and knots.

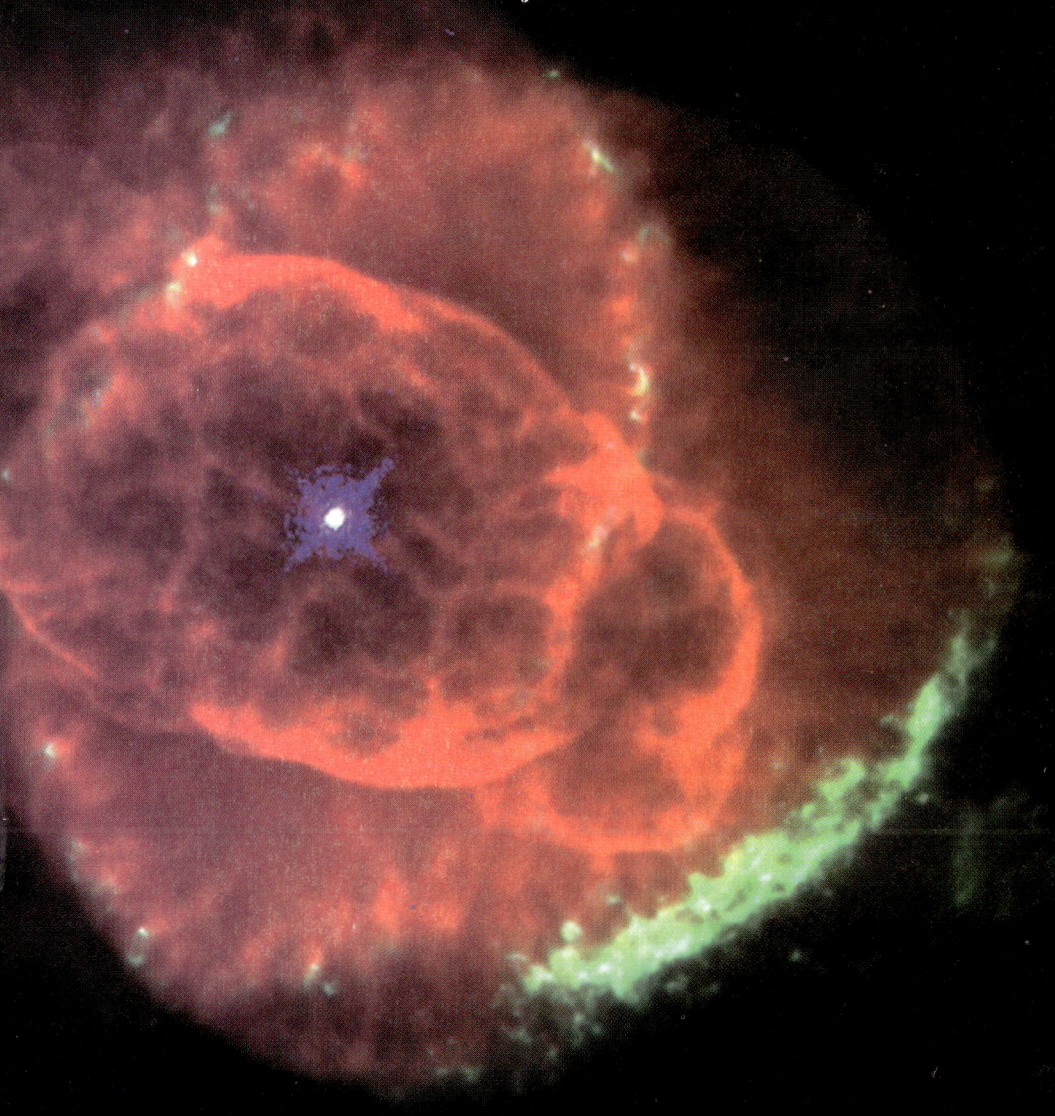

NGC 2440

LINK TO EARTH
Distance: 3,600 ly
Constellation: Puppis
RA: 7:42 hr
DEC: -18.3 deg
Brightness: 11th mag

Did You Know

that you can see the clear form of a butterfly with outstretched wings in this cloud? This is a beautiful illusion created by dark, cool dust between you and the nebula's core.

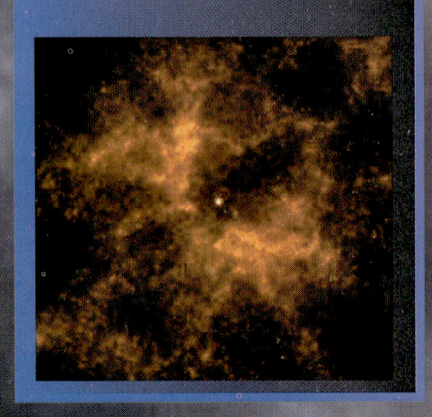

56

Approaching

Sadly you realize that this is the atmosphere of a star near death. Gravity has compressed and heated the old stellar core and made it the hottest star known, with a surface temperature of over 200,000°C.

Up Close

You'll be surprised by the messy appearance of this ghost cloud. Its unusual shape comes from the violent explosions that created it.

Eventually the cloud's central star will shrink to the size of Earth and gradually cool — or if the star continues to collapse, it could disappear from our universe as a black hole.

Hourglass Nebula

LINK TO EARTH
Distance: 8,000 ly
Constellation: Antlia
RA: 13:39 hr
DEC: -67.4 deg
Brightness: 14th mag

Did You Know

that each of these beautiful colors is produced by gas at a different temperature? Brighter colors show hotter regions close to the central star. Cooler outer regions are dark orange. Arcs on the outside make it look like we could jump into the hourglass funnels. But this gas is really moving outward — away from the "eye" in the center.

Approaching

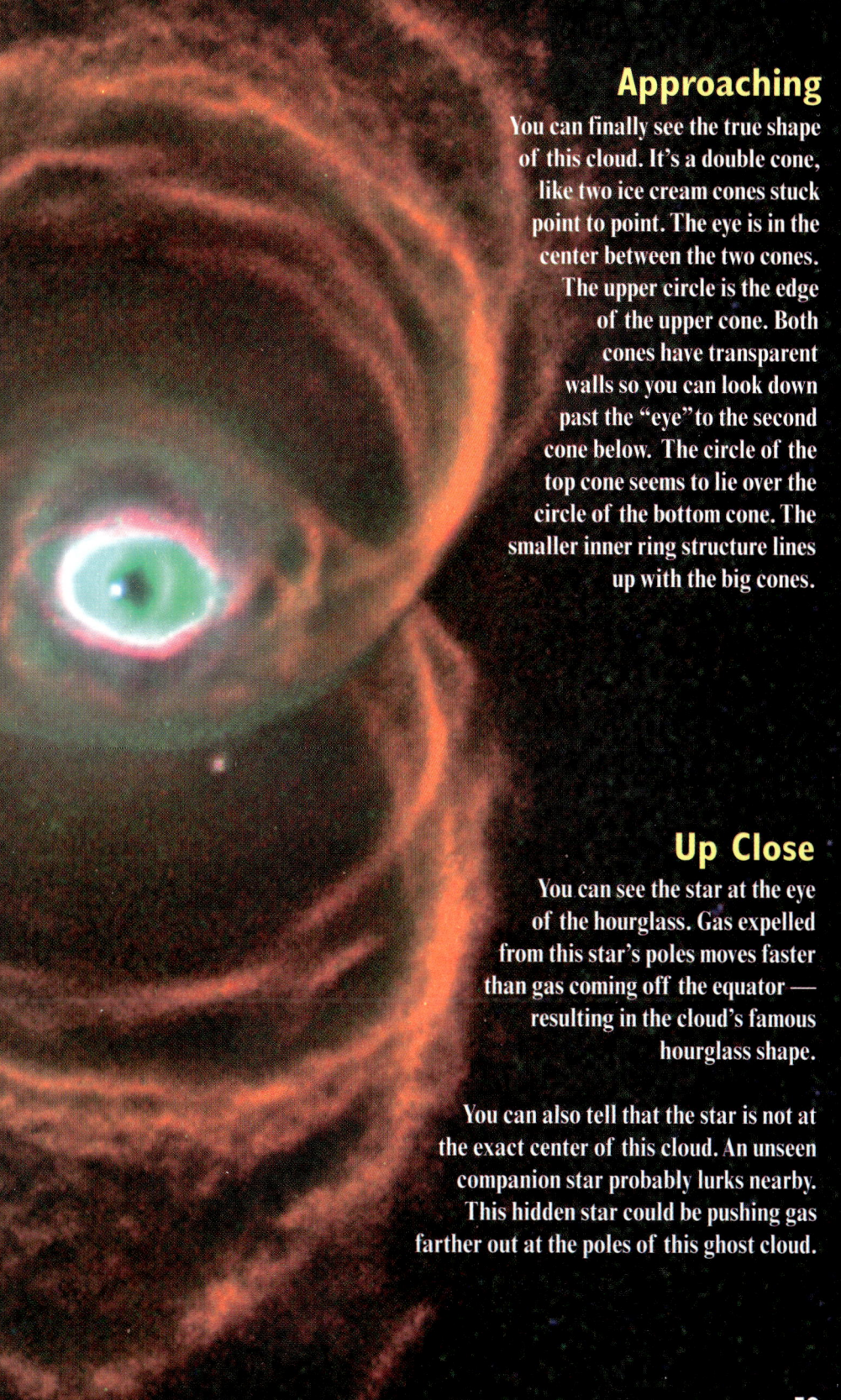

You can finally see the true shape of this cloud. It's a double cone, like two ice cream cones stuck point to point. The eye is in the center between the two cones. The upper circle is the edge of the upper cone. Both cones have transparent walls so you can look down past the "eye" to the second cone below. The circle of the top cone seems to lie over the circle of the bottom cone. The smaller inner ring structure lines up with the big cones.

Up Close

You can see the star at the eye of the hourglass. Gas expelled from this star's poles moves faster than gas coming off the equator — resulting in the cloud's famous hourglass shape.

You can also tell that the star is not at the exact center of this cloud. An unseen companion star probably lurks nearby. This hidden star could be pushing gas farther out at the poles of this ghost cloud.

NGC 2346

LINK TO EARTH
Distance: 2,000 ly
Constellation: Monoceros
RA: 7:09 hr
DEC: -0.8 deg
Brightness: 12th mag

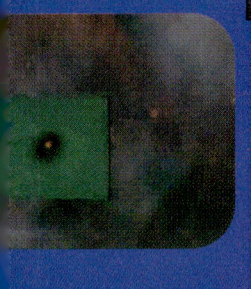

Did You Know

that a murder happened here? A pair of stars lies at the center of this cloud. They spin around each other in a death dance — so close together that they circle every 16 days. One is the hot core of the old star that produced these butterfly wing clouds. When this star expanded to become a red giant, it actually swallowed its smaller companion star.

Approaching

Now you can tell more about the murder that once occurred here. When the bigger star engulfed its companion, the cores of the two stars began to spiral together. This caused the ejection of the outer layers of the cannibal red giant. Most of the atmosphere became a dense glowing disk, which hides the central stars now.

Up Close

You can "feel" a fast stellar wind coming from the hot cannibal star. This wind has inflated the two large, wispy butterfly wings, extending out from the disk. The total diameter of this nebula is about one-third of a light-year, or two trillion miles.

Minkowski 2-9

Did You Know

that some ghost clouds are like the exhaust of a super-sonic jet airplane? In fact, this cloud looks like a pair of jet engine exhausts.

LINK TO EARTH
Distance: 2,100 ly
Constellation: Ophiuchus
RA: 17:05 hr
DEC: -10.1 deg
Brightness: 15th mag

Approaching

Watch the motion in the gas jets. They're blowing at over 200 miles per second and causing this whole cloud to expand. The stellar outburst that formed these gas lobes occurred just 1,200 years ago.

Up Close

The central stars here are a very close pair. In fact, one star may have swallowed the other. The gravity of the more massive star pulls gas from the atmosphere of the other star and flings it into a thin, dense disk. This gas doughnut surrounds both stars and extends into space to about ten times the diameter of Pluto's orbit around the sun.

This dense disk causes the jet-like shape of the cloud. A high-speed wind from one of the stars rams into the disk which funnels the hot gas into the pair of jets you see. In this image, oxygen glows red and blue while nitrogen is green.

The ghost clouds that you have seen on this tour represent the fate of your sun in about five billion years.

Tour 4 Grave- yards

Connection

The largest and heaviest stars burn hotter, faster, and at the end of their lives, explode violently. This tour visits the most famous star graveyards with bright lighthouses and hidden whirlpools.

Before exploding, these massive stars are bright-red supergiants in the top right of the star diagram. After exploding, the hot stellar remnant glows very faintly in visible light and lies near the bottom of the diagram.

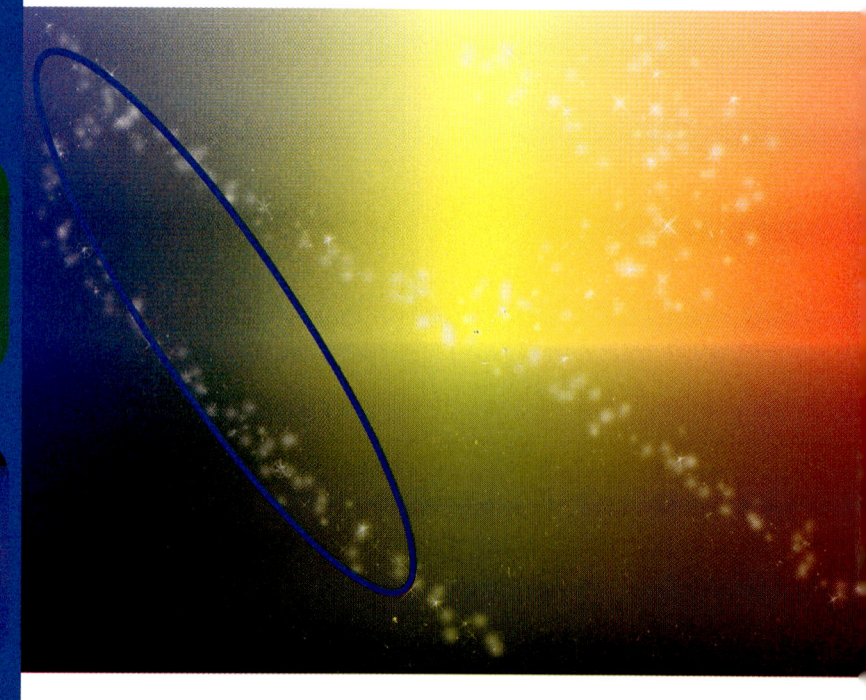

After a star explodes, the core remains behind while the star's atmosphere flies away. In this core, all protons and electrons have been squeezed together into neutrons and packed as tightly as possible. A neutron star with more mass than the sun might be only ten miles wide. These collapsed neutron stars spin very rapidly—often hundreds of turns every second!

Graveyards

Tour Briefing

Neutron stars also produce beams of radio waves that sweep across the sky as the star spins. If you are lined up with a beam, the star will seem to blink on and off as the beam crosses in front of you, like a lighthouse beacon. For this reason, these stars are also called pulsars.

Be careful when coming close to collapsed stars because the trail of a dying star may lead you to a star that explodes or to a gravity vortex called a black hole.

This picture shows the remains of a star 3,000 years after it exploded in the Large Magellanic Cloud. Gas from the dead star rushes outward at 2,000 kilometers per second and crashes into cool neighboring clouds. Blue-green oxygen-rich clouds come from the star's core. Filaments of the cool surrounding gas glow pink from the collisions.

This supernova remnant, called N132D, contains heavy elements made inside the dead star. Elements like carbon and oxygen are needed for life like yours to form.

Super-
nova
1987A

LINK TO EARTH
Distance: 169,000 ly
Constellation: Doradus
RA: 5:35 hr
DEC: -69.2 deg
Brightness: 4th mag

Did You Know

that astronomers saw a star explode in 1987? This star lies beyond the Milky Way Galaxy in a small neighboring galaxy about 140,000 light-years from Earth.

Suddenly the star became very bright – outshining the rest of its galaxy. It has been slowly fading since this explosion.

The top flip movie shows the cloud patterns around the explosion. The bottom flip movie depicts the actual explosion.

Approaching

Notice the cloudy shapes nearby. The surrounding nebula is complex and beautiful, but not directly related to the supernova.

As you come closer, you can see the main center ring. This material was ejected in a flat disk thousands of years before the main explosion.

Up Close

Study the two fainter rings carefully. These aren't really rings, but two cones. When you look into the cones, you can see the gas in the walls. The cones are too thin for you to see when you look sideways through the walls.

Imagine you could fly around the supernova cloud. Flip Movie D carries you all around and shows the cones clearly. Notice how the cones of glowing gas show up as rings when you look directly into the cone.

1987A part 2

LINK TO EARTH
Distance: 169,000 ly
Constellation: Doradus
RA: 5:35 hr
DEC: -69.2 deg
Brightness: 5th mag

Did You Know

that supernova 1987A became 10,000 times brighter in just two weeks?

Approaching

The outer rings have been expanding for thousands of years and are floating out into space very slowly.

The inner material was shot away by the recent incredible explosion. Soon these fast-moving gases will catch up and collide with the outer material. Look for evidence of this as you approach.

The row at the bottom of the screen shows a series of pictures of the central star. Look how much this object changed in two years.

Up Close

Oxygen, nitrogen, hydrogen, and other gases rush toward you and away from the center of the explosion at 30,000 kilometers per hour.

When these gases hit the outer, slower-moving material, the collision creates heat and the gas begins to glow. These exploding stars spread heavy elements all over space.

Feb. '94   Sept. '94   Mar. '95   Feb. '96

Nova Cygni 1992

Approaching

Compare the picture on the right, taken about a year ago, with how the star looks now. Notice that the bar is fading away and the overall shape is becoming less circular. There must be hidden material here which is acting like a girdle to hold in the expanding ring.

LINK TO EARTH
Distance: 10,430 ly
Constellation: Cygnus
RA: 20:30 hr
DEC: 52.5 deg
Brightness: 5th mag

Did You Know

that a nova or "new star" appeared in the constellation Cygnus in 1992? Although nova means new star, this is really a very old, white dwarf that has collected enough material on its surface to ignite.

White dwarfs are very dense, with the mass of the sun packed into a ball the size of the Earth. They are also among the hottest stars, sometimes over 100,000°C. When gas falls onto a white dwarf, the gas becomes very hot and unstable. Eventually the gas explodes violently. These explosions continue as long as material falls onto the star.

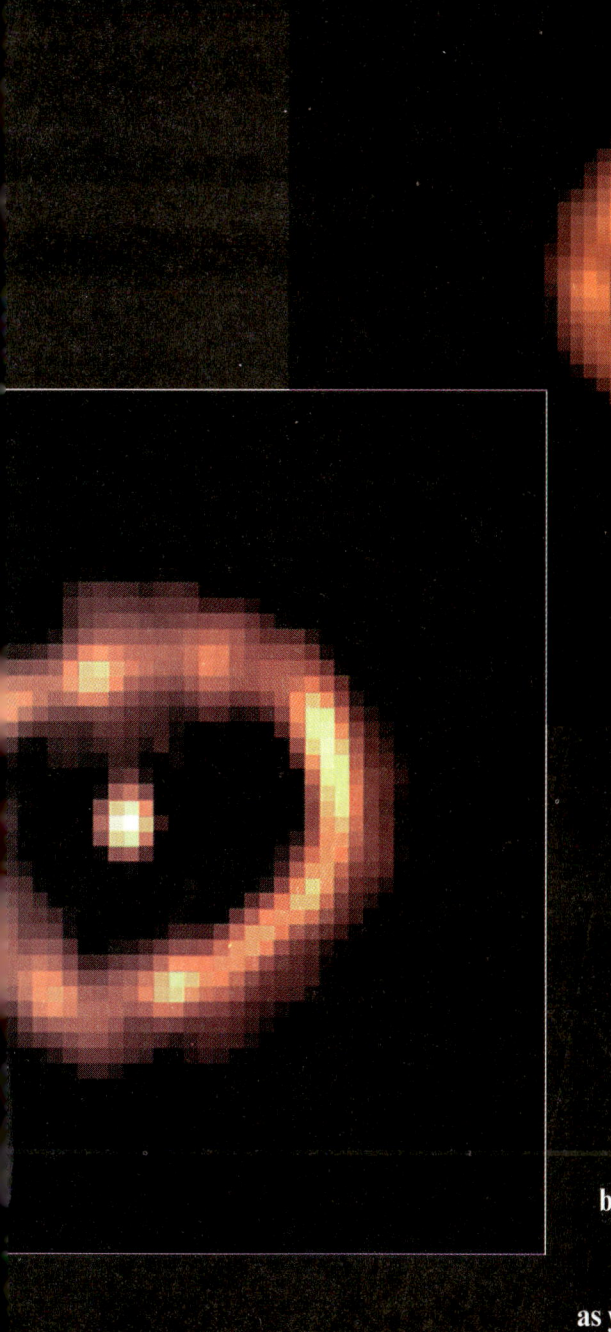

Up Close

There may be another star hiding behind the dark clouds at the center and the ring of dust may also hide planets. Look for this second star as you fly toward Nova Cygni 1992. If you see it, you will be the first Earthling to know for certain what is going on in this star system.

Crab Nebula

LINK TO EARTH
Distance: 7,000 ly
Constellation: Taurus
RA: 5:34hr
DEC: 22 deg
Brightness: 8th mag

Did You Know

that Chinese astronomers saw a star appear in 1054? It was so bright that they could see it in the daytime. They observed and recorded the star as did the Anasazi who lived in the area that is now New Mexico.

Stars that are old and very massive have fused some of their lighter elements into heavier ones like oxygen. In supernova explosions even heavier elements, like iron, are formed.

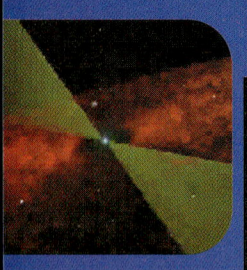

Approaching

You can see different gases as you approach the Crab Nebula. Each glows in its own colors. For thousands of years after the explosion, this cast-off material will radiate energy from the initial explosion. Then finally it will fade into darkness.

Up Close

Expanding gases and dust cool off and grow fainter and fainter. These gases move through empty space until they collect as part of a new dusty cloud. This new cloud may collapse into a new star and planetary system.

The sun and Earth, and everything on the Earth, came from a cloud with heavy elements that were created in a supernova explosion long ago.

Crab Nebula Pulsar

LINK TO EARTH
Distance: 7,000 ly
Constellation: Taurus
RA: 5:34 hr
DEC: 22 deg
Brightness: 8th mag

Did You Know

that the star in the center of the Crab Nebula blinks? The remnant of this supernova explosion is a tiny, very dense neutron star or pulsar. It spins around 30 times every second and sends powerful radio beams flashing through space. These powerful emissions also light up the surrounding cloud.

Up Close

These arcs are lit up by the energy from the spinning pulsar. The pulsar slings away particles at close to the speed of light. This is by far the most dangerous place you have visited. Be careful and don't go too close.

The bottom flip movie shows the pulsar's spinning light beam.

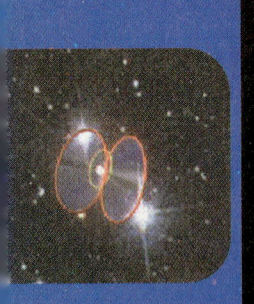

Approaching

The star in the center is the neutron star. The arcs around it create the illusion of a mysterious eye. As you watch, you can see these arcs expanding away from the central star. Three pictures taken a few days apart clearly show the movement here in the center of the Crab Nebula.

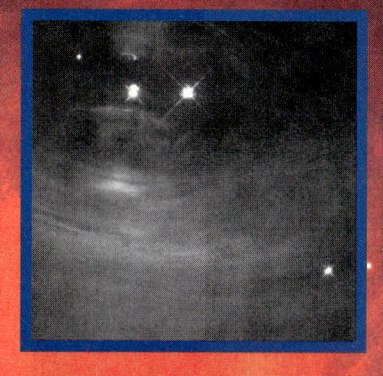

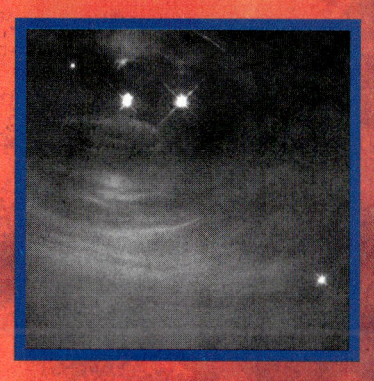

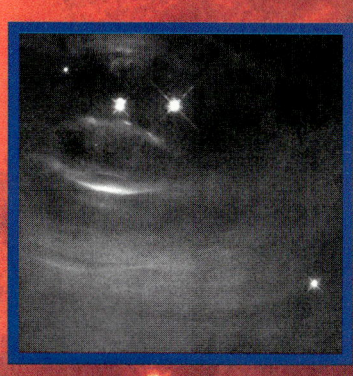

Cygnus loop

Approaching

Long ago a very bright star with a strong wind cleared out a huge bubble around it. Fifteen thousand years ago, this giant star exploded inside the empty cavity it had created. Now the powerful shock wave from the explosion has reached the surrounding cloud.

For as long as the pyramids of ancient Egypt have marked the tombs of long-dead pharaohs, the wispy threads of this supernova have marked the grave of the long-dead star.

LINK TO EARTH
Distance: 2,500 ly
Constellation: Cygnus
RA: 20:51 hr
DEC: 30.7 deg
Brightness: 8th mag

Did You Know

that the Cygnus loop covers a huge part of Earth's sky? The loop is a rough circle with a diameter six times larger than the full moon.

A supernova exploded here over 15,000 years ago. Since then, the cloud has expanded into space in large gaseous arcs and loops.

Up Close

Dropping a rock in a very still pond can create ripples that disturb water far away. In the same way, this explosion is still shaking up a region 130 light-years across 15,000 years later. The supernova's heavy elements will become part of future solar systems.

For a close encounter with these smashing clouds, explore the mystery image at the beginning of the book.

77

Tour 5
Cosmic Villages

Connection

All stars in a cluster formed at about the same time from the same cloud, but some of the stars grew larger than others. This difference in mass has caused stars to be at different places on the star diagram. More massive stars are brighter and hotter and evolve into red giants more quickly.

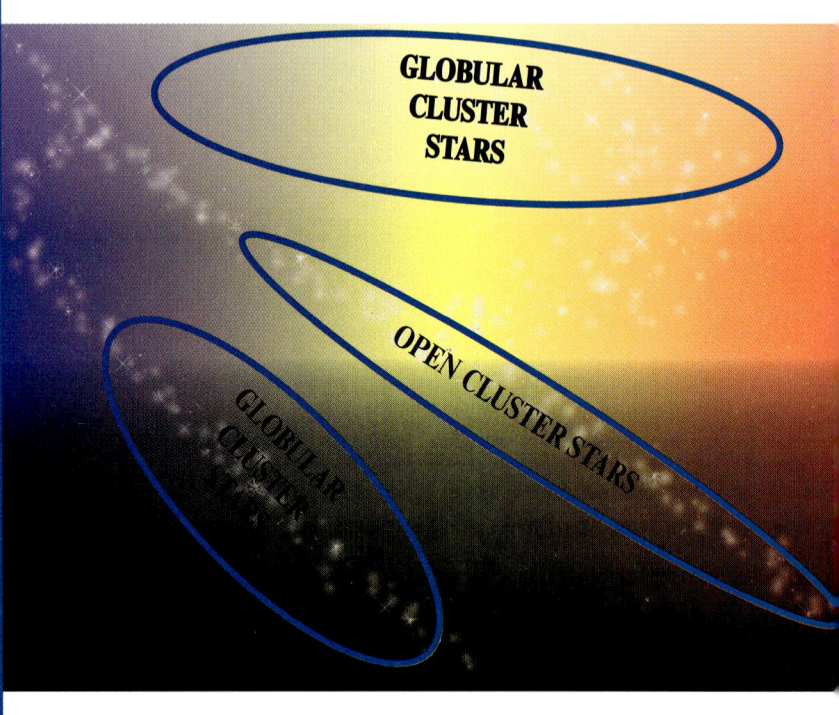

GLOBULAR CLUSTER STARS

OPEN CLUSTER STARS

GLOBULAR CLUSTER STARS

Many of the stars in older globular clusters have left the center of the diagram and evolved into red giants and white dwarfs.

Most of the stars in the younger, open clusters are along the line in the center of the diagram. These stars are middle-aged, like the sun. Only a few very massive stars in an open cluster have turned into giants. Open clusters are not as old as the globulars.

In this tour you will explore both kinds of clusters.

Cosmic Villages

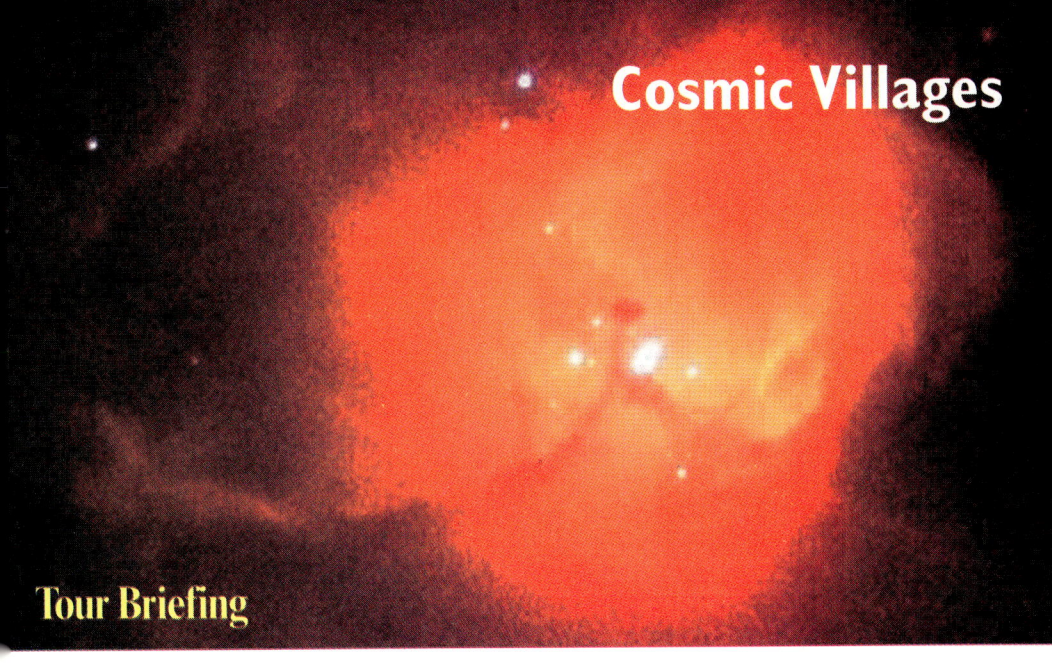

Tour Briefing

Many stars form in clusters – either loose, open clusters or tightly-packed, globular clusters.

There are more than a thousand open clusters in the Milky Way Galaxy. Stars in open clusters are much like the sun – containing about 90% hydrogen, 9% helium, and less than 1% other elements.

Open clusters contain from tens to hundreds of stars and are often surrounded by clouds of gas and dust. You will find open clusters in the spiral arms of a galaxy.

In contrast, globular clusters contain thousands of stars packed very close together in a spherical shape without any surrounding dust. A globular has fewer stars on the outside with stars more closely-packed in the center. You will find globulars above and below the galactic plane in a region surrounding the galaxy's core called the galactic halo.

Members of globular clusters were the first stars born as the galaxy formed. The old stars in these clusters are almost entirely hydrogen and helium with less than 1% other elements.

In the cluster above, you see very bright stars lighting up the surrounding gas. These super-hot stars pour out gas at a furious rate and create dramatic shapes in the cloud's glowing gases.

This young cluster lies in the neighboring galaxy called the Small Magellanic Cloud. It provides a rare close-up of the violence that accompanies the birth of very massive stars.

Each of these stars shines with the brilliance of 300,000 suns. Clusters of hot, young stars were much more common billions of years ago when star formation began in the universe.

M4

LINK TO EARTH
Distance: 7,000 ly
Constellation: Scorpius
RA: 16:24 hr
DEC: -26.5 deg
Brightness: 6th mag

Did You Know

that the nearest globular cluster to Earth is M4 – over 7,000 light-years away with more than 100,000 stars? This cluster is 47 light-years across.

You could come here to see what the Sun will look like in the distant future when it becomes a white dwarf.

80

Approaching

In the M4 globular cluster, you can look for dying white dwarf stars. In this small area, notice the white dwarfs (inside the circles) scattered among the cluster's much brighter population of yellow, sunlike stars and cooler, red dwarfs. By comparing a yellow star with a white dwarf, you can see how much your sun will change when it dies about five billion years from now.

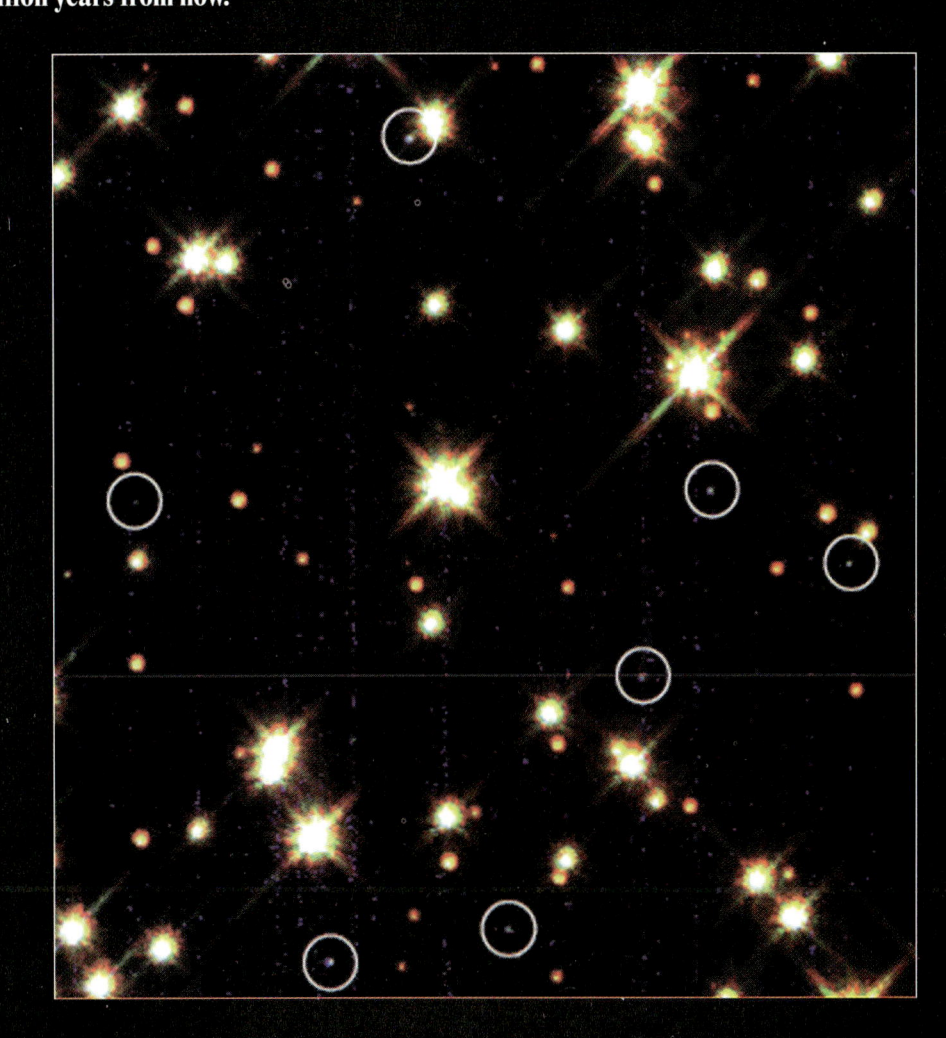

Up Close

If you search the entire cluster, you'll find about 40,000 white dwarfs. These stars no longer use nuclear fusion to make energy. Instead they give off light as they cool and collapse. Astronomers use the temperatures of these stars to predict how long it takes for white dwarfs to cool off and to figure out that the universe must be over 10 billion years old.

M15

LINK TO EARTH
Distance: 50,000 ly
Constellation: Pegasus
RA: 21:30 hr
DEC: 12.2 deg
Brightness: 8th mag

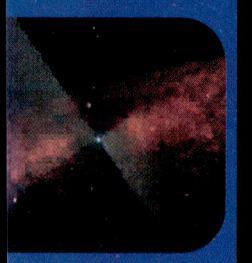

Did You Know

that the most closely-packed globular cluster in the Milky Way Galaxy contains several million stars?

You're exploring the core of this cluster to find a massive black hole or a "core collapse" caused by the intense gravitational pull of so many stars in such a small space.

Approaching

Your view of the whole cluster is about 28 light-years across. The image below shows the innermost 1.6 light-years. The hottest stars appear blue, while the coolest stars are reddish-orange. The stars are much closer together near the cluster's center.

Up Close

At some point in the distant past, the stars converged on M15's core, like bees swarming to their hive. This runaway collapse may have lasted a few million years – a flash in the 12-billion-year life of the cluster. A precise reading of the speeds at which stars move near M15's core will reveal whether the stars are packed so tightly because of the influence of a single massive object or simply by their own mutual attraction. Stars would orbit more quickly in the gravitational grip of a black hole. Thus far no one has located a black hole here.

NGC 6397

LINK TO EARTH
Distance: 7,500 ly
Constellation: Ara
RA: 17:40 hr
DEC: -53.6 deg
Brightness: 6th mag

Approaching

The 200 stars in this cluster are so spread out that you can see distant background galaxies behind them.

Did You Know

that astronomers look for tiny red dwarfs in globular clusters? If the dark matter in our galaxy was made of faint red stars, then about 38 such stars should have been visible in this tiny part of a globular cluster. The simulated stars (diamond-shaped symbols) show what you would have seen if these faint red stars actually existed. But the red dwarfs aren't there. These surprising results rule out dim stars as an explanation for the missing dark matter in the Milky Way Galaxy.

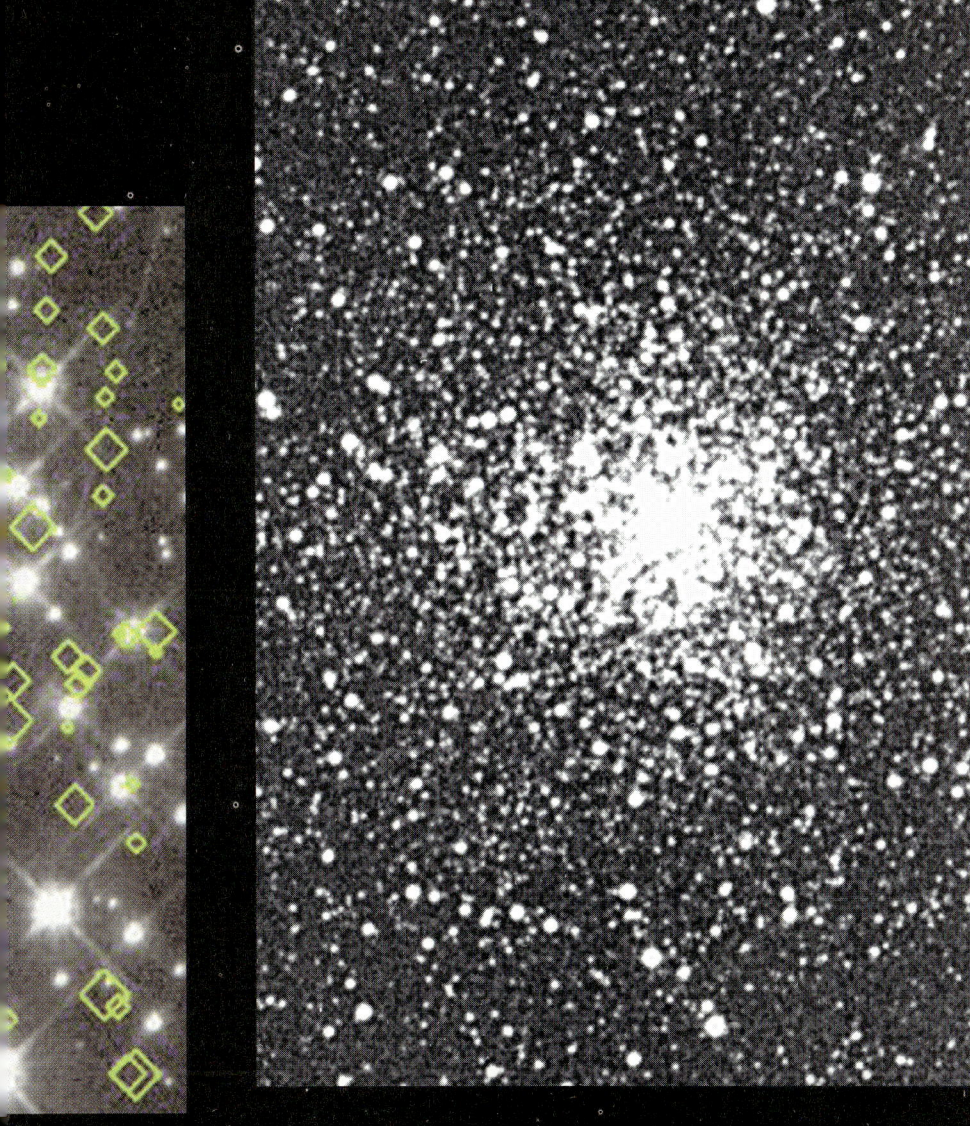

Up Close
By observing this galaxy, scientists have identified a surprising cutoff point for star formation. Nature apparently doesn't make many stars smaller than a fifth of the mass of your sun. If there were lower mass stars in this cluster, then this image would contain 300 more stars.

47 Tucanae

LINK TO EARTH
Distance: 15,000 ly
Constellation: Tucana
RA: 0:15 hr
DEC: -72.1 deg
Brightness: 5th mag

Did You Know

that by peering into the heart of this globular cluster's bright core, you can separate the dense clump into many different individual stars?

Approaching

The core of globular cluster 47 Tucanae is home to many blue stragglers. These are rejuvenated stars glowing with the blue light of young stars. Blue stragglers are formed either by the slow merge of stars in a double-star system or by the collision of two unrelated stars.

Up Close

Filters bring out the colors of the different stars in the crowded core of this cluster. Through this window red giant stars appear orange, sunlike stars are white/green, and the strange blue stragglers look blue.

NGC 1818

LINK TO EARTH
Distance: 164,000 ly
Constellation: Doradus
RA: 5:04 hr
DEC: -66.4 deg
Brightness: 10th mag

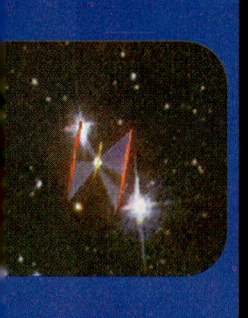

Did You Know

that some rich star clusters look like jewel boxes in the sky? The thousands of stars in the NGC 1818 cluster shimmer like precious gems in a myriad of sizes and colors.

Approaching

This young cluster is only 40 million years old, compared with five billion years for the age of your sun. These young stars are so bright that you can see them at a distance of 164,000 light-years. The cluster belongs to the neighboring Large Magellanic Cloud.

Up Close

This rich cluster makes an ideal laboratory for studying how stars change. Here astronomers have found a very young white dwarf with a sizzling surface temperature of 30,000°C. This star formed from a red giant very recently. To have evolved so quickly, the star must once have been over seven times the sun's mass.

And this is a mystery. How could so large a star turn into a small white dwarf? Astronomers expected a star this big to explode, yet the star just faded away.

G1/M31
Mayall II

LINK TO EARTH
Distance: 2.4 million ly
Constellation: Andromeda
RA: 0:33 hr
DEC: 39.5 deg
Brightness: 10th mag

Did You Know

that the brightest globular cluster in the Local Group of galaxies orbits the neighboring Andromeda Galaxy? Named G1 or Mayall II, it contains at least 300,000 old stars. The Local Group consists of about 20 nearby galaxies, including the Milky Way.

Approaching

Andromeda is the nearest major spiral galaxy to your Milky Way. G1 is located 130,000 light-years from Andromeda's nucleus. The fainter helium-burning stars have temperatures and brightnesses like those of the oldest clusters in the Milky Way Galaxy. This cluster must, therefore, be about the same age as your galaxy's oldest clusters.

Up Close

This cluster was probably formed shortly after the beginning of the universe. It provides astronomers with a record of the earliest era of star formation.

NGC 1850

LINK TO EARTH
Distance: 166,000 ly
Constellation: Doradus
RA: 5:08 hr
DEC: -68.5 deg
Brightness: 10th mag

Did You Know

that sometimes you can see one cluster in front of another? Here you see a pair of star clusters 166,000 light-years away in the Large Magellanic Cloud. The Large Magellanic Cloud is a small companion galaxy belonging to the Milky Way.

Approaching

This field of view is 130 light-years across with nearly 10,000 stars. Most of these stars belong to the dominant yellow cluster called NGC 1850, which is about 50 million years old. The nearby cluster of white stars is only about four million years old. These are two separate star groups lying along the same line of sight. The younger white cluster is 200 light-years farther away than the older yellow cluster. The red stars belong to the background of the Large Magellanic Cloud.

Up Close

It is very unusual to find two well-defined clusters so close together. Perhaps supernova explosions in the older cluster triggered the birth of the younger cluster. Gas expelled at high speed from the older cluster collided with other gas and caused star formation. In this view, yellow stars correspond to stars like our sun; red stars are cool giants and supergiants; white stars are hot young stars that produce a lot of ultraviolet light.

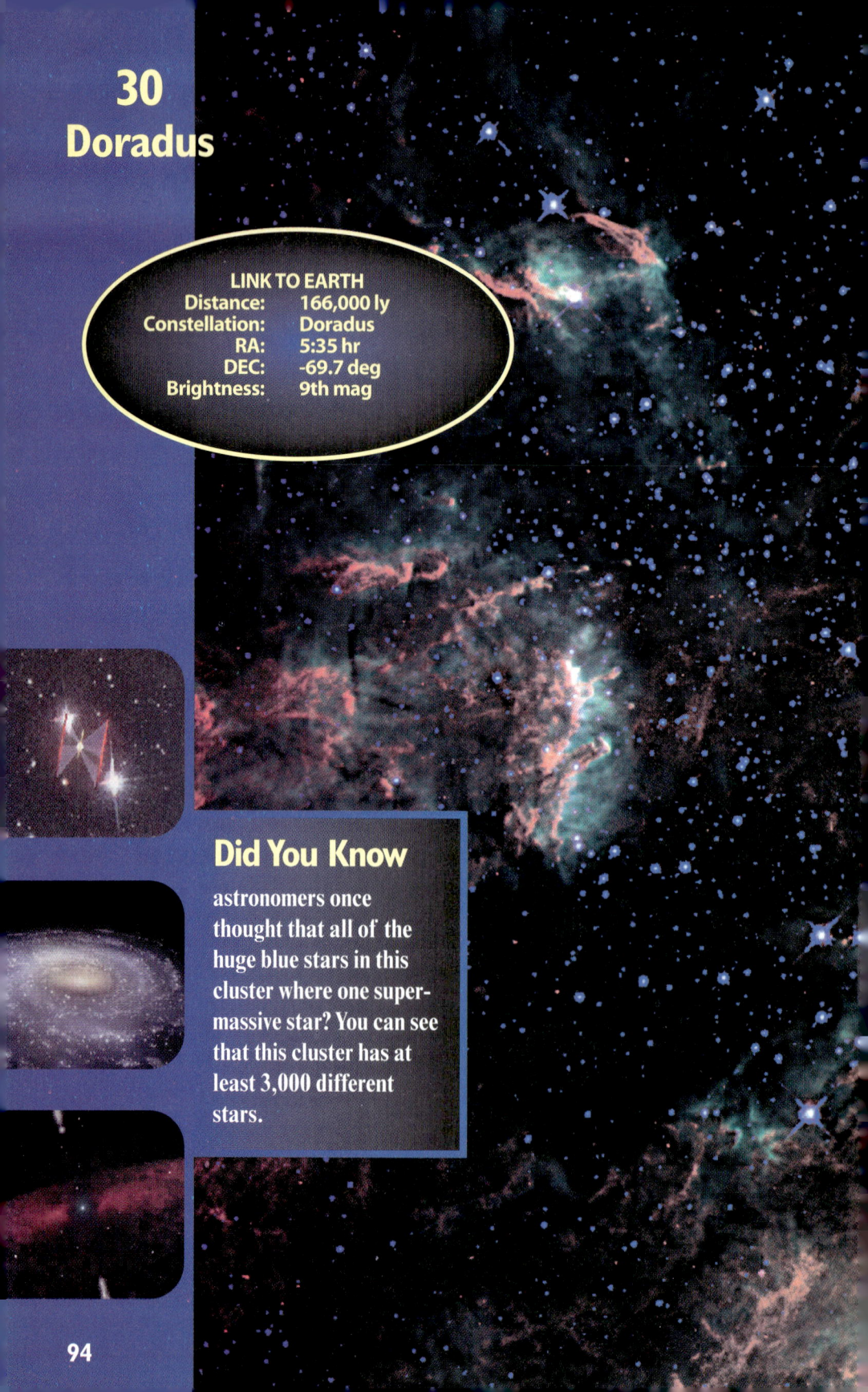

30 Doradus

LINK TO EARTH
Distance: 166,000 ly
Constellation: Doradus
RA: 5:35 hr
DEC: -69.7 deg
Brightness: 9th mag

Did You Know

astronomers once thought that all of the huge blue stars in this cluster where one super-massive star? You can see that this cluster has at least 3,000 different stars.

Approaching

The star cluster lies at the heart of the 30 Doradus Nebula, which is also called the Tarantula Nebula — perhaps because it looks like a giant spider from a distance. This nebula belongs to the neighboring Large Magellanic Cloud. It's unusual because so much gas has turned into massive, hot blue stars which cause a huge portion of the nebula to glow.

Up Close

This star cluster is very young — only a few million years old. Its hot young stars have not had time to evolve. Just look at all of these stars — each producing millions of times more energy than your sun. You are very lucky to be here to see this infant star cluster before its biggest stars begin to grow old.

Tour 6
Island Hopping

Connection

The hazy Milky Way band stretches across Earth's night sky. This is the disk of your home galaxy – a spiral-shaped island of over a hundred billion stars. The sun and solar system lie on the inside of one of the galaxy's spiral arms, about half-way out from the galaxy's center.

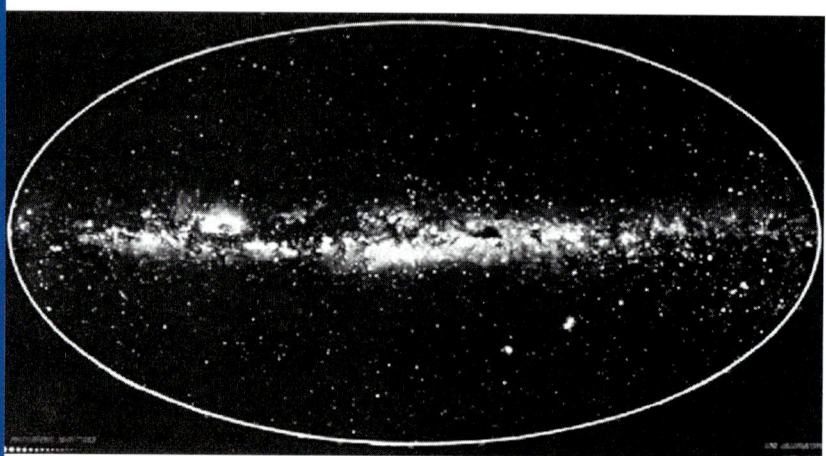

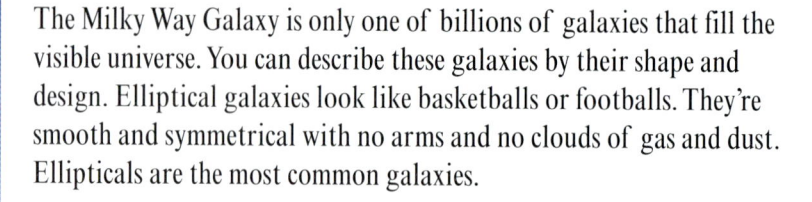

The Milky Way Galaxy is only one of billions of galaxies that fill the visible universe. You can describe these galaxies by their shape and design. Elliptical galaxies look like basketballs or footballs. They're smooth and symmetrical with no arms and no clouds of gas and dust. Ellipticals are the most common galaxies.

Spirals are the most beautiful and familiar galaxies. There are two distinct kinds of spirals – normal spirals and barred spirals. Normal spirals, like the Milky Way, have arms winding outward from opposite sides of the galaxy's core. In barred spirals, the arms emerge from the ends of a straight bar passing through the galaxy's center. For both kinds of spirals, bright gaseous knots and clusters of hot young stars lie along the arms. Older stars live in the central regions and flattened disk.

About three percent of all galaxies are irregulars – blobs of stars, gas, and dust with no distinct shape. Irregular galaxies have lots of bright blue stars, star clusters, and gas clouds.

Island Hopping

Tour Briefing

You can see several star generations in the center of the Whirlpool Galaxy (M51), a nearby spiral with an irregular companion galaxy. This galaxy's massive center is 80 light-years across and has a brightness of 100 million suns.

This galaxy is your first stop on the Island Hopping tour. Here you'll look for standard candles – or stars whose brightness we already know. With these standard stars, astronomers can estimate how far away this galaxy is.

At each island galaxy, you'll look for a familiar star or star cluster that you can use to judge the distance from home.

The spiral arms of M51 are huge bands of stellar birth clouds. These stars shine brightly and cause the arms to stand out against the background of older stars in the galaxy's disk.

Star formation in these arms is caused by a density wave that travels around the disk and triggers star birth in a spiral pattern. Most spiral galaxies have two prominent arms, but you may discover a galaxy with only one arm or with three.

As you explore this galaxy, you may also find the mysterious black hole that lies at the galaxy's heart.

M51

LINK TO EARTH
Distance: 23 million ly
Constellation: Canes Venatici
RA: 13:30 hr
DEC: 47.2 deg
Brightness: 10th mag

Did You Know

that a dwarf companion galaxy passed through the Whirlpool Galaxy about 400 million years ago and triggered the formation of young stars near the galaxy's center?

98

Approaching

Surrounding the center of this galaxy is a halo of stars that are at least eight billion years old and perhaps as old as the universe itself. This halo is normal, but just beyond it is a necklace of infant stars less than 10 million years old. Normally, young stars are born far from the galaxy's center – out in its spiral arms. These stars were probably created by the collision with the dwarf galaxy.

Up Close

The sky never gets dark near the center of this galaxy. The concentration of stars here is about 5,000 times higher than in your solar neighborhood.

SN 1994I

Approaching

The inner region of the Whirlpool Galaxy's spiral disk extends all the way into its bright nucleus. An arrow points to the location of the supernova, 2,000 light-years from the nucleus. When this supernova exploded, it became a billion times brighter than the sun.

LINK TO EARTH
Distance: 23 million ly
Constellation: Canes Venatici
RA: 13:30 hr
DEC: 47.2 deg
Brightness: 10th mag

Did You Know

that astronomers can estimate the brightness of an exploding supernova — even in a distant galaxy? Once they know how bright an object really is, they can compare this brightness with what the object looks like in the sky. The lower the object's apparent brightness, the farther away the object is. A bright supernova called 1994I told astronomers that the Whirlpool Galaxy is 23 million light-years away.

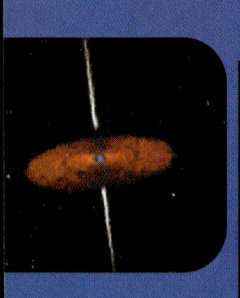

Up Close (Supernova)

This supernova lies in front of a diffuse background of starlight so you can see the ejected clouds. A violent supernova explosion destroys the star and ejects the elements created by the star's nuclear fusion into the gas between stars. Your Earth is formed from elements created in ancient supernova explosions in your own Milky Way Galaxy.

Up Close

Notice the dark, dusty "Y" across the galaxy's center. The bright dot in the middle of the "Y" is as bright as a million suns, but is less than five light-years wide. You've found this galaxy's elusive central black hole and the source of powerful radio jets. The light comes from glowing matter rushing toward the black hole.

M100

Approaching

M100 is a spiral galaxy in the huge Virgo Cluster of 2,500 galaxies (the nearest large cluster of galaxies).

From the brightness of the throbbing Cepheid variable stars in this galaxy, astronomers have determined that this galaxy is 56 million light-years from Earth. Since M100 is in the Virgo Cluster, the whole cluster must be at the same distance.

LINK TO EARTH
Distance: 60 million ly
Constellation: Coma Berenices
RA: 12:23 hr
DEC: 15.9 deg
Brightness: 10th mag

Did You Know

that stars called Cepheids throb like giant hearts? These stars expand and contract and expand and contract with a regular beat every few weeks — and change brightness in the process. The time between expansions indicates how bright the Cepheid really is. So astronomers time pulsing Cepheids and observe how bright they look in a distant galaxy. Since they know how bright the Cepheid really is, they can estimate how far away its galaxy is. The two pictures below show stars in a tiny part of a spiral arm of M100. The star that changed brightness is a Cepheid.

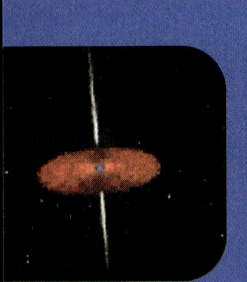

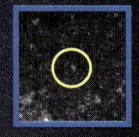

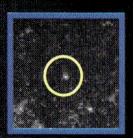

Up Close

M100 is a majestic, face-on spiral galaxy, similar to your Milky Way. Notice the middle-aged stars along with clouds of gas, dust, and new stars in this galaxy's spiral arms. Astronomers in M100 would see a similar view if they looked at your neighborhood of the Milky Way.

NGC 253

LINK TO EARTH
Distance: 8 million ly
Constellation: Sculptor
RA: 0:47 hr
DEC: -25.3 deg
Brightness: 8th mag

Did You Know

that there is a population explosion in some spiral galaxies, like NGC 253? Here new stars are being born at a frantic rate – much faster than in the Milky Way. The cause of these starbursts remains a mystery.

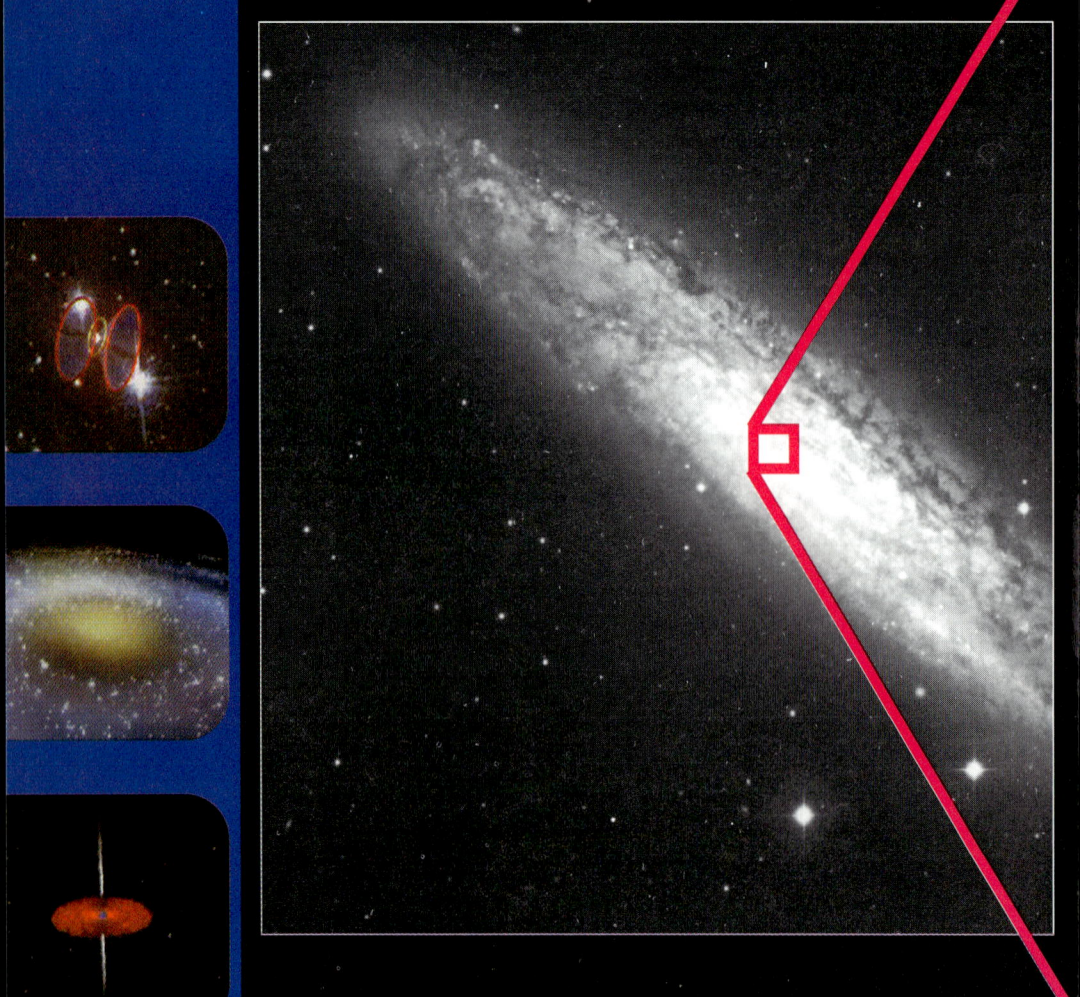

Approaching

This is the core of the nearest starburst spiral galaxy, NGC 253. Here you can watch violent star formation within a region 1,000 light-years across. Look carefully for complex structures in this galaxy's core, including brilliant star clusters and dust lanes.

Up Close

Follow these dust lanes to trace out regions of glowing gas and newborn stars. You can almost feel the stars being born from the heat produced by the warm dust surrounding them.

These regions of intense star formation include a bright, super-compact star cluster. Stars are often born in these dense clusters within starbursts. By coming this close, you can peer through some of the dense gas that obscures the starburst core.

NGC 1365

LINK TO EARTH
Distance: 60 million ly
Constellation: Fornax
RA: 3:33 hr
DEC: -36.1 deg
Brightness: 10th mag

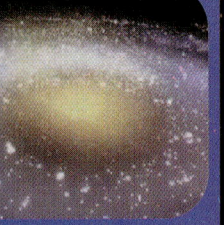

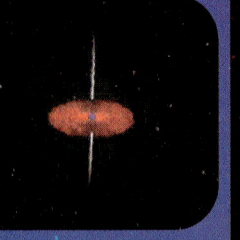

Did You Know

that some spiral galaxies have a distinct "bar" of stars, dust, and gas across the center? These barred spirals are more rare than normal spirals, like your Milky Way Galaxy.

Approaching
NGC 1365 is a barred spiral galaxy located in the Fornax Cluster of galaxies. The line of small blue dots shows where stars are forming in the galaxy's spiral arms, making them ideal targets for the discovery of Cepheids.

Up Close
Astronomers have discovered about 50 Cepheids here – each throbbing at its own rate and shining at its own brightness. From these Cepheids, astronomers know that this galaxy is just 60 million light-years from Earth.

NGC 1808

Approaching

You can see that NGC 1808 is a barred spiral galaxy with stars forming on both sides of the bright nucleus. Gases streaming along the bar toward the center may be causing a burst of star formation.

LINK TO EARTH
Distance: 40 million ly
Constellation: Columba
RA: 5:07 hr
DEC: -37.5 deg
Brightness: 10th mag

Did You Know

that a galaxy can be warped with curls of gas and dust at its outer spiral arms?

This warp may come from a close encounter with another galaxy.

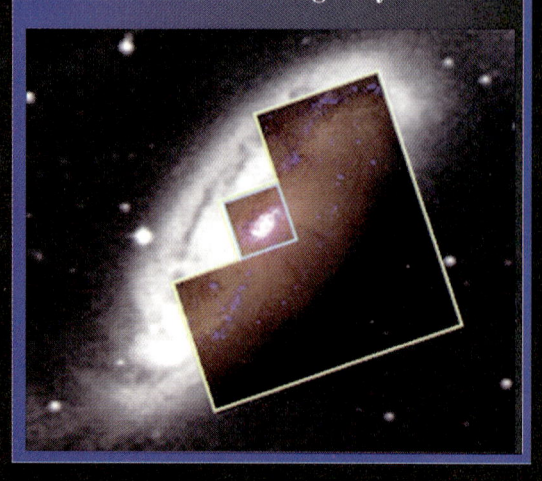

108

Up Close

Supernovas at the galaxy's center send filaments of dust flying from the starburst region.

The brightest knot of star birth is probably a giant cluster of stars about 100 light-years across at the very center of the galaxy. To the right is a close-up view of the galaxy's center.

NGC 4314

LINK TO EARTH
Distance: 40 million ly
Constellation: Coma Berenices
RA: 12:22 hr
DEC: 29.8 deg
Brightness: 11th mag

Approaching

Outer spiral arms form from the ends of the bar which runs through the center of this galaxy. All is quiet here. Very little happens out this far from the galaxy's core. It's a good place to raise a solar system with planets.

In this galaxy, the fast lane is a ring circling the galaxy's center. Here you can see rich clusters of newborn stars created within the last five million years. Your sun is a thousand times older than these baby stars. This stellar ring is a laboratory where you can investigate how new stars form. The bluish-purple patches in the ring are clusters of infant stars. Two dark dust lanes and a pair of thin blue spiral arms surround the ring.

The large bar of stars running through the galaxy's center pushes the dust lanes into the ring. There young star clusters trap the dust and use it to fuel more star formation. The blue spiral arms contain teenage stars, less than 200 million years old. Although young compared with your sun, these stars are much older than the baby stars in the ring.

Did You Know

that a galaxy with a bar through its center can also have a ring? This bright ring is 1,000 light-years wide and surrounds the galaxy's core. This is where most of the new stars in the galaxy are forming.

Up Close

This galaxy has something for everyone. Just look at the core. Here you'll find dust lanes and even a small bar of stars. Miniature spiral arms have also formed around the ring. It's like a miniature galaxy within a galaxy.

This galaxy is special. You can find dust lanes in the cores of many galaxies, but not tiny spiral arms full of hot young stars.

Colors are very important here. Blue indicates hot wasteful newborn stars. White and yellow stars are much calmer and older. Dark areas show where dust clouds hide. Glowing hydrogen gas, excited by nearby stars, produces the purple color.

NGC 4881

LINK TO EARTH
Distance: 314 million ly
Constellation: Coma Bernices
RA: 12:59 hr
DEC: 28.3 deg
Brightness: 14th mag

Did You Know

that astronomers make pictures of fields of galaxies? You can see younger, closer galaxies in front of older, more distant ones.

Up Close

Many globular clusters surround NGC 4881. By comparing the apparent brightness of these globular clusters with their real brightness, astronomers estimate that NGC 4881 is more than 300 million light-years away. The whole Coma Cluster must also be this far away.

The distance to the Coma Cluster is an important cosmic yardstick for scaling the size of the universe. Astronomers know that NGC 4881 is moving away from the Milky Way Galaxy at a rate of 21,000 light-years per second. Since we know how far away this galaxy is, we now have a measure of the expansion rate for the whole universe (70 light-years per second per million light-years away).

Explore the background for other interesting galaxies. At the top right is a beautiful face-on spiral. You can also see a galaxy collision in progress. Some of these galaxies belong to the Coma Cluster and others are even more distant.

Approaching

The brightest object in your field is NGC 4881, an elliptical galaxy in the outskirts of the Coma Cluster. Unlike spiral galaxies, ellipticals have used up most of their supplies of gas and can no longer form new stars. This great cluster of galaxies contains at least a thousand bright galaxies – mostly spirals and ellipticals.

NGC 7252

LINK TO EARTH
Distance: 126 million ly
Constellation: Aquarius
RA: 22:20 hr
DEC: -24.6 deg
Brightness: 12th mag

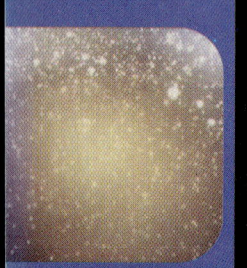

Did You Know

that some galaxies are so unusual that astronomers call them "peculiar"? NGC 7252 is one of these galaxies. Peculiar galaxies can have distorted shapes and bright bridges of gas and dust.

Approaching

The central galaxy in this image is four billion light-years away. The reddish arc to the lower right is the farthest object from Earth ever seen. The light from the galaxy behind has been traveling for 93% of the age of the universe. Lensing by the center galaxy makes this galaxy bright enough for us to see it.

Up Close

As you zoom in, you can find the smeared, reddish arc. The arc's bright patches are regions of star formation while the dark patches are dusty clouds. You are seeing what one very young galaxy looked like as it formed over 13 billion years ago.

143

Glossary Guide

Special Places

If you're looking for a specific destination, use this guide.

Black Hole: An object collapsed by gravity until its gravitational pull is so strong that nothing, not even light, can travel fast enough to escape.
Tour 7: pages 124 - 131

Brown Dwarf: A star-like object that is too small to make its own energy by fusing hydrogen into helium. Telescopes that can "see" infrared radiation (like the Hubble Space Telescope) can detect brown dwarfs.
Tour 2: pages 32 - 37

Galaxy: A group of billions of stars and often gas held together by gravity.
Tour 6: pages 96 - 123
Spiral Galaxies have bright arms with gas and dust clouds where new stars are forming.
Spiral galaxies on pages 96 - 111, 114 - 115
Elliptical Galaxies do not have arms or star–forming regions.
Elliptical galaxies on pages 112 - 113
Colliding Galaxies are moving through each other and causing rapid star formation in their wake.
Colliding galaxies on pages 116 - 123

Galaxy Cluster: Group of galaxies held together by gravity
Tour 6: pages 112-113

Gravitational Lens: When light from a distant object is bent by the gravitational pull of another galaxy, a gravitational lensing effect may cause us to see many images of the distant object.
Tour 7: pages 138 - 143

Jets of Gas: These are produced by very young stars and black holes.
Tour 1: pages 28 - 31, Tour 7: pages 126 - 131

Nebula: A cloud of dust and gas. Nebulas (or nebulae) are bright, glowing clouds lit up by the hot new stars within or thrown off by old stars. Nebulas are the birth places or graveyards of stars.
Tour 1: pages 14 - 27, Tours 3 and 4: 48 - 77

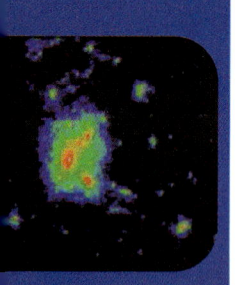

Neutron Star (Pulsar): Collapsed star core composed of neutrons. It produces a pulse of light as it spins.
  Tour 4: pages 64 - 65, 72 - 75

Nova: Component of a close, double-star system that explodes and becomes hundreds of times brighter.
  Tour 4: pages 70 - 71

Planetary Nebula: At the end of a star's life, its outer layers are blown away, creating a shell of dust and gas around the star. This shell is called a planetary nebula.
  Tour 3: pages 46 - 63

Proplyd: A proto-planetary disk – found in young gas clouds.
  Tour 1: pages 22 - 23

Quasars: Distant galaxies which give out incredible energy.
  Tour 7: pages 130 - 131

Red Dwarf : Star that is less massive and cooler than the sun.
  Tour 2: pages 32 - 35, Tour 5: pages 84-85

Red Giant : An old star expands as it starts to fuse helium as well as hydrogen. This expansion cools the surface of the star and it becomes a red giant.
  Tour 2: pages 32 - 33, 44 - 45

Star: An object that is hot enough in its center to fuse hydrogen into helium.
  Tour 2: pages 32 - 45

Star Cluster: Group of hundreds or thousands of stars held together by gravity.
  Tour 5: pages 78 - 95

Supernova: A massive dying star that violently ejects its outer layers in an explosion that makes the star thousands of times brighter.
  Tour 4: pages 66 - 69, 76 - 77

White dwarf: The core of a dying star that remains after the outer layers have been ejected. While dwarfs collapse down until they have a diameter only a little larger than the Earth's and slowly cool.
  Tour 2: pages 32 - 33, Tour 5: 80-81

Image Credits

Special People

Each day research astronomers using the Hubble Space Telescope make new discoveries about new places in the universe. These new images appear on the Internet website for the Space Telescope Science Institute — http://www.stsci.edu. Visit this website to continue exploring the universe.

The following astronomers, designers, and spacecraft researchers have made this book possible. Their efforts in capturing images and interpreting them have resulted in the beautiful pages that fill the Earthlings Guide. Each image reflects the excitement and enthusiasm of the person listed below who captured it and reproduced it for us to enjoy.

Welcome to the Universe:

W. Freedman (Carnegie Observatories) and NASA, pp. 1, 3, 13
Solar and Heliospheric Observatory, ESA and NASA, pp. 2, 9
Galileo Mission, JPL, NASA, pg. 2
Apollo 17 crew, JSC, NASA, pg. 2
Voyager Mission, JPL, NASA, pg. 2
A. Dupree (CfA) and NASA, pp. 2, 13
A. Caulet (ST-ECF, ESA) and NASA, pp. 3, 13
J.P. Harrington and K.J. Borkowski (University of Maryland) and NASA, pp. 3,13
R. Gilmozzi (STScI/ESA), Shawn Ewald (JPL) and NASA, pp. 3, 13
Key observing project (STScI) and NASA, pg. 3
Matt Bobrowsky (Orbital Sciences Corporation), NASA, pg. 4
Space Based Astronomy, Gregory L. Vogt, NASA, pg. 5
Hubble Space Telescope pictures, National Space Science Data Center, pp. 6, 7
Jeff Hester and Paul Scowen (Arizona State University) and NASA, pg. 8, 15-17
Laurent Drissen, Jean-Rene Roy and Carmelle Robert (Department de Physique and Observatoire du mont Megantic, Universite Laval), Yvan Dutil/ CFHT and NASA, pg. 9
HR Diagram, Carrie Presley, Avela, pg. 10
Gary Young, Avela, pg. 11
Jeff Hester and Paul Scowen (Arizona State University) and NASA, pg. 13
L. Ferrarese (Johns Hopkins University) and NASA, pg. 13

Tour 1:
Playgrounds
>HR Diagram, Carrie Presley, Avela, pg. 14
>
>Jeff Hester and Paul Scowen (Arizona State University) and NASA, pp. 15-17
>
>A. Caulet (ST-ECF, ESA) and NASA, pp. 18-19
>
>C. Robert O'Dell, Shui Kwan Wong (Rice University) and NASA, pp. 20-23
>
>Rodger Thompson, Marcia Rieke, Glenn Schneider, Susan Stolovy (University of Arizona), Edwin Erickson (SETI Institute/Ames Research Center), David Axon (STScI) and NASA, pp. 24-25
>
>Hui Yang (University of Illinois) and NASA, pp. 26-27
>
>J. Morse (STScI) and NASA, pp. 28-29
>
>J. Hester (Arizona State University), the WFPC 2 Investigation Definition Team and NASA, pp. 30-31

Tour 2:
Star Hopping
>HR Diagram, Carrie Presley, Avela, pg. 32
>
>Andrea Dupree (Harvard-Smithsonian CfA), Ronald Gilliland (STScI), NASA and ESA, pg. 33
>
>C. Barbieri (Univ. of Padua) and NASA/ESA, pp. 34-35
>
>D. Golimowski (Johns Hopkins University) and NASA, pp. 34-35
>
>T. Nakajima and S. Kulkarni (Caltech), S. Durrance and D. Golimowski (JHU) and NASA, pp. 36-37
>
>Al Schultz (CSC/STScI) and NASA, pp. 38-39
>
>Rodger Thompson, Marcia Rieke and Glenn Schneider (University of Arizona) and NASA, pp. 40-41
>
>Don F. Figer (UCLA) and NASA, pp. 42-43
>
>Jon Morse (University of Colorado) and NASA and ERO program, pp. 44-45

Tour 3:
Ghost Clouds
>HR Diagram, Carrie Presley, Avela, pg. 46
>
>Bruce Balick (University of Washington), Jason Alexander (University of Washington), Arsen Hajian (U.S. Naval Observatory), Yervant Terzian (Cornell University), Mario Perinotto (University of Florence, Italy), Patrizio Patriarchi (Arcetri Observatory, Italy) and NASA, pg. 47
>
>C. Robert O'Dell and Kerry P. Handron (Rice University), NASA, pp. 48-49
>
>H. Bond (STScI) and NASA, pp. 50-51

Image Credits

R. Sahai and J. Trauger (JPL), the WFPC2 Science Team and NASA, pg. 52

Rodger Thompson, Marcia Rieke, Glenn Schneider, Dean Hines (University of Arizona); Raghvendra Sahai (Jet Propulsion Laboratory); NICMOS Instrument Definition Team and NASA, pp. 52-53

J.P. Harrington and K.J. Borkowski (University of Maryland) and NASA, pp. 54-55

S. R. Heap (GSFC) and NASA, pg. 56

H. Bond (STScI), R. Ciardullo (PSU) and NASA, pp. 56-57

R. Sahai and J. Trauger (JPL), the WFPC2 Science Team and NASA, pp. 58-59

Massimo Stiavelli (STScI) and NASA, pp. 60-61

Bruce Balick (University of Washington), Vincent Icke (Leiden University, The Netherlands), Garrelt Mellema (Stockholm University) and NASA, pg. 62-63

Tour 4:
Graveyards

HR Diagram, Carrie Presley, Avela, pg. 64

Jon A Morse (STScI) and NASA, pg. 65

P. Challis (CfA) and NASA, pp. 66-67

Chun Shing Jason Pun (NASA/GSFC), Robert P. Kirshner (Harvard-Smithsonian Center for Astrophysics) and NASA, pp. 68-69

F. Paresce, R. Jedrzejewski (STScI) NASA/ESA, pp. 70-71

Jeff Hester and Paul Scowen (Arizona State University) and NASA, pp. 72-75

Jeff Hester (Arizona State University) and NASA, pp. 76-77

Tour 5:
Cosmic Villages

HR Diagram, Carrie Presley, Avela, pg. 78

Mohammad Neydari–Malayeri; (Paris Observatory, France), NASA/ESA, pg. 79

J. Hester (Arizona State University), the WFPC 2 Investigation Definition Team, and NASA, pp. 80-81

P. Guhathakurta (UCO/Lick Observatory, UC Santa Cruz), B. Yanny (Fermi National Accelerator Lab), D. Schneider

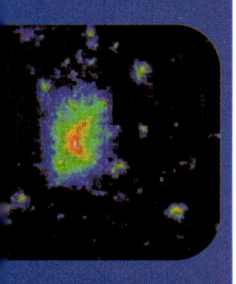

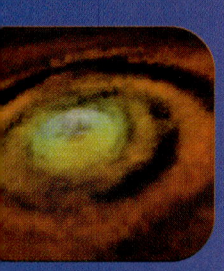

(Pennsylvania State Univ.), J. Bahcall (Inst. for Advanced Study) and NASA, pp. 82-83

F. Paresce, STScI /ESA and NASA, pp. 84-85

R. Saffer (Villanova University), D. Zurek (STScI) and NASA, pp. 86-87

Rebecca Elson and Richard Sword, Cambridge UK, and NASA(Original WFPC2 image courtesy J. Westphal, Caltech), pp. 88-89

Michael Rich, Kenneth Mighell, and James D. Neill (Columbia University), Wendy Freedman (Carnegie Observatories) and NASA, pp. 90-91

R. Gilmozzi (STScI/ESA), Shawn Ewald (JPL) and NASA, pp. 92-93

Early Release Observation STScI and NASA, pp. 94-95

Tour 6:
Island Hopping

Lund Observatory, Sweden, pg. 96

Nino Panagia (STScI/ESA) and NASA, pp. 97-99

Robert P. Kirshner/Harvard-Smithsonian Center for Astrophysics and NASA, pp. 100-101

Nino Panagia (STScI/ESA) and NASA, pg. 101

J. Trauger (JPL) and NASA, pp. 102-103

W. Freedman (Carnegie Observatories) and NASA, pp. 102-103

Jay Gallagher (University of Wisconsin-Madison), Alan Watson (Lowell Observatory, Flagstaff, AZ) and NASA, pp. 104-105

W. Freedman (Carnegie Observatories), the Hubble Space Telescope Key Project team and NASA, pp. 106-107

Jim Flood, an amateur astronomer affiliated with Sperry Observatory at Union College in New Jersey, and Max Mutchler, a member of the STScI staff, pp. 108-109

G. Fritz Benedict, Andrew howell, Inger Jorgensen, David Chapell (University of Texas), Jeffery Kenney (Yale University), and Beverly J. Smith (CASA, University of Colorado), and NASA, pp. 110-111

William A. Baum, Astronomy Department University of Washington, and Hubble Space Telescope WFPC Team, pp. 112-113

B. Whitmore (STScI) and NASA, pp. 114-115

William Keel and Raymond White (University of Alabama in Tuscaloosa) and NASA, pp. 116-117

Rodger Thompson, Marcia Rieke, Glenn Schneider (University of Arizona) and Nick Scoville (California Institute of Technology) and NASA, pp. 118-119

Kirk Borne (ST ScI) and NASA, pp. 120-121

Brad Whitmore (STScI) and NASA, pp. 122-123

Image Credits

Tour 7:
In the Distance

Key observing project (STScI) and NASA, pp. 124, 136-137

Roeland P. van der Marel (STScI), Frank C. van den Bosch (Univ. of Washington), and NASA, pg. 125

E. Schreier (STScI) WFPC2, NOAO/CTIO, Jack O. Burns (University of Missouri), David Clarke (St. Mary's University, Nova Scotia), and NASA, pp. 126-127

Philippe Crane (European Southern Observatory) and NASA, pp. 128-129

L. Ferrarese (Johns Hopkins University) and NASA, pp. 130-131

Holland Ford, STScI/Johns Hopkins University; Richard Harms, Applied Research Corp.; Zlatan Tsvetanov, Arthur Davidsen, and Gerard Kriss at Johns Hopkins; Ralph Bohlin and George Hartig at STScI; Linda Dressel and Ajay K. Kochhar at Applied Research Corp. in Landover, Md.; and Bruce Margon from the University of Washington in Seattle, pp. 132-133

John Bahcall (Institute for Advanced Study, Princeton), Mike Disney (University of Wales), pp. 134-135

Kavan Ratnatunga (Johns Hopkins University) and NASA, pp. 138-139

W.N. Colley and E. Turner (Princeton University), J.A. Tyson Technologies) and NASA, pp. 140-141

Marijn Franx (University of Groningen, The Netherlands), Garth Illingworth (University of California, Santa Cruz) and NASA, pp. 142-143

Flipbooks:

(throughout book)
B C. Burrows and J. Krist (STScI) and NASA
F Edmund Bertschinger (MIT), NASA
STScI and NASA

Front and End Pages:

Bruce Balick (University of Washington), Vincent Icke (Leiden University, The Netherlands), Gerrelt Mellema (Stockholm University) and NASA, pg. i

Jeff Hester (University of Arizona), NASA, pg. iii

Key observing project (STScI) and NASA, pg. v

National Space Science Data Center, pg. 151

**A special thanks to the astronauts
who maintain the Hubble Space Telescope**

Star Map

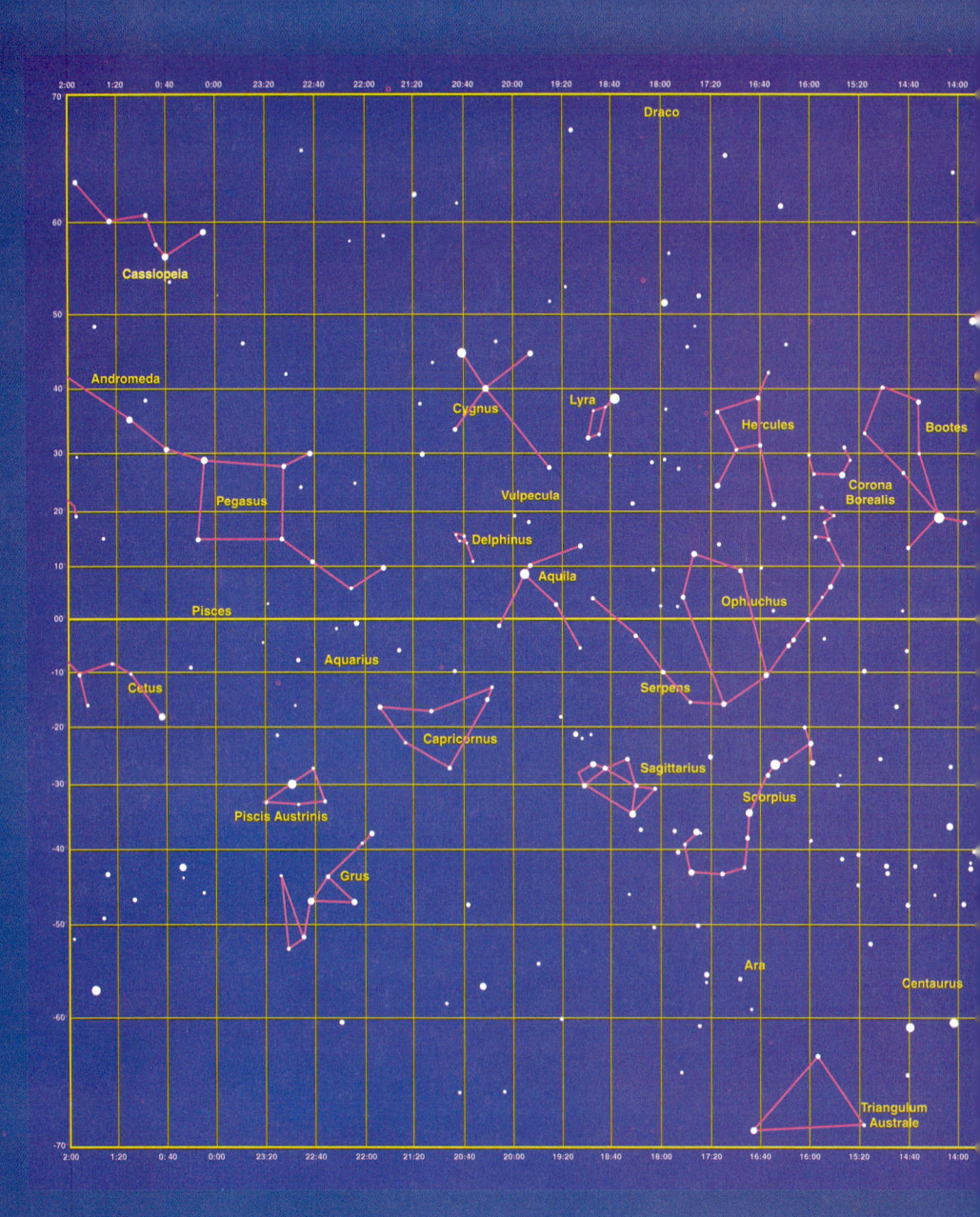

153

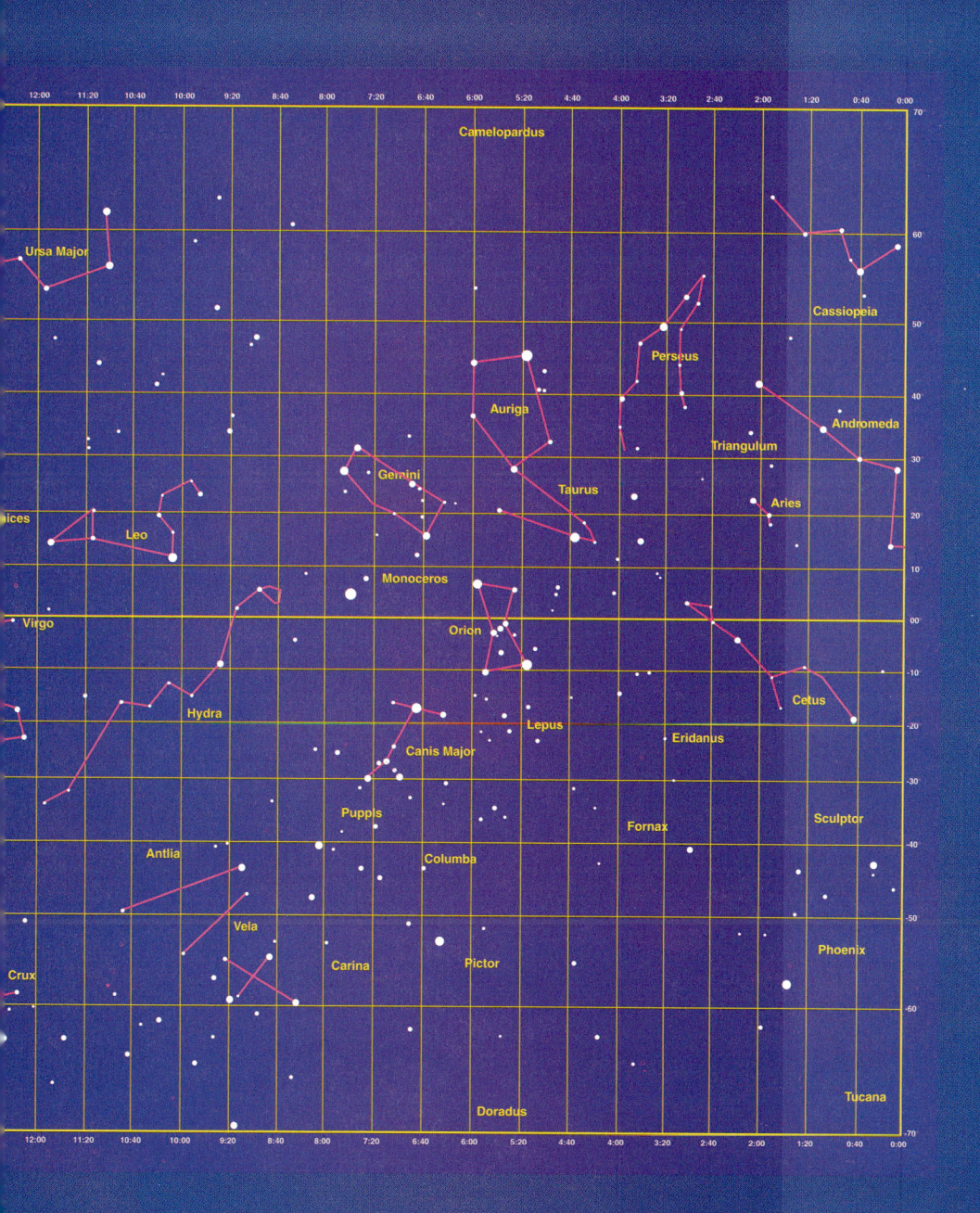